3/93

What Uncle Sam Really Wants

Noam Chomsky

Odonian Press
Berkeley, California

The material in this book was compiled from the following talks and interviews. Dr. Chomsky then made extensive additions, deletions and changes to the edited draft.

- A talk included in a teach-in on WBAI radio in New York City on January 13, 1991

- A telephone interview conducted by Kris Welch and Philip Maldari on KPFA radio, Berkeley, California on December 12, 1990

- *The Sociopolitical Context of the Assassination of Ignacio Martín-Baró*, a talk given on August 13, 1990 at the annual meeting of the American Psychological Association in Boston

- *US Still at War Against the World*, an article (excerpted from a talk given to the Central America Solidarity Association) published in the May, 1990 issue of the *Resist* newsletter

- Interviews conducted by David Barsamian in Cambridge, Massachusetts on February 1 and 2, 1990

- *The Roots of US Intervention*, a talk given at Lewis & Clark College in Portland, Oregon on January 24, 1989, and the question-and-answer period following

- *United States International and Security Policy: The "Right Turn" in Historical Perspective*, a talk given at the University of Colorado at Boulder on October 22, 1986, and the question-and-answer period following

---

Chomsky, Noam
    What Uncle Sam really wants / Noam Chomsky.
        p. cm. — (Real story)
    Includes bibliographical references (p.) and index.
    ISBN 1-878825-01-1 : $5.00
    1. United States—Foreign relations—Philosophy. 2. United States—Foreign relations—1945–1989. 3. United States—Foreign relations—1989- I. Title. II. Series: Real story (Berkeley, Calif.)
E183.7.C48   1992
327.73—dc20   92-23824
                                      CIP

Printed in the United States of America   Second printing, Nov. 1992

327.73
CHO

Additional copies of this book and others in the Real Story series are available for $5 + $2 shipping per *order* (not per book) from Odonian Press, Box 7776, Berkeley CA 94707. Please write for information on quantity discounts, or call us at 510 524 3143. Distribution to book stores and wholesalers is through Publishers Group West, Box 8843, Emeryville CA 94662, 510 658 3453 (toll-free: 800 788 3123).

Original materials: David Barsamian

Additional transcription: Women's Empowerment Project

Compilation: Arthur Naiman

Editing: Arthur Naiman, Sandy Niemann

Copy-editing and proofreading: Karen Faria, Sandy Niemann, Susan McCallister, Christine Carswell, John Kadyk

Inside design and page layout: Arthur Naiman

Production coordination: Karen Faria

Index: Michael Brackney, Marc Savage

Printing: Michelle Selby, Jim Puzey / Consolidated Printers, Berkeley, California

Nontoxic editing refuge: Miriam Finkel

Moral support and emotional triage: Linda Spangler

Series editor: Arthur Naiman

Series coordinator: Susan McCallister

Odonian Press gets its name from Ursula Le Guin's wonderful novel *The Dispossessed* (though we have no connection with Ms. Le Guin or any of her publishers). The last story in her collection *The Wind's Twelve Quarters* also features the Odonians.

Odonian Press donates at least 10% (last year it was 36%) of its aftertax income to organizations working for social justice.

Contents

Brainwashing at home

The future

Editors' foreword

Noam Chomsky is a major figure in twentieth-century linguistics. Born in Philadelphia in 1928, he's taught since 1955 at the Massachusetts Institute of Technology, where he became a full professor at the age of 32.

In addition to his work as a linguist, Chomsky has written many books on contemporary issues. His political talks have been heard, typically by standing-room-only audiences, all over the country and the globe.

In a saner world, his tireless efforts to promote justice would have long since won him the Nobel Peace Prize, but the committee keeps giving it to people like Henry Kissinger.

If you're used to thinking of the United States as the defender of democracy throughout the world, you'll find much of what you read in this book incredible. But Chomsky is a scholar; the facts in this book are just that, and every conclusion is backed by massive evidence (see pp. 103-105 for references to some of it).

It was *very* hard to compress the vast sweep of Chomsky's social thought into so small a book. You'll find a list of his other political books, which cover the topics introduced here in infinitely greater detail, on p. 102.

Hundreds of tapes and transcripts of Chomsky's talks and interviews (and those of many other interesting speakers) are available from David Barsamian, 2129 Mapleton, Boulder CO 80304, 303/444-8788 (free catalog on request).

Arthur Naiman, Sandy Niemann

The main goals of US foreign policy

Protecting our turf

Relations between the United States and other countries obviously go back to the origins of American history, but World War II was a real watershed, so let's begin there.

While most of our industrial rivals were either severely weakened or totally destroyed by the war, the United States benefited enormously from it. Our national territory was never under attack and American production more than tripled.

Even before the war, the US had been by far the leading industrial nation in the world—as it had been since the turn of the century. Now, however, we had literally 50% of the world's wealth and controlled both sides of both oceans. There'd never been a time in history when one power had had such overwhelming control of the world, or such overwhelming security.

The people who determine American policy were well aware that the US would emerge from WW II as the first global power in history, and during and after the war they were carefully planning how to shape the postwar world. Since this *is* an open society, we can read their plans, which were very frank and clear.

American planners—from those in the State Department to those on the Council on Foreign Relations (one major channel by which business leaders influence foreign policy)—agreed that the dominance of the United States had to be maintained. But there was a spectrum of opinion about how to do it.

At the hard-line extreme, you have documents like National Security Council Memorandum 68 (1950). NSC 68 developed the views of Secretary of State Dean Acheson and was written by Paul Nitze, who's still around (he was one of Reagan's arms-control negotiators). It called for a "roll-back strategy" that would "foster the seeds of destruction within the Soviet system," so that we could then negotiate a settlement on our terms "with the Soviet Union (or a successor state or states)."

The policies recommended by NSC 68 would require "sacrifice and discipline" in the United States—in other words, huge military expenditures and cutbacks on social services. It would also be necessary to overcome the "excess of tolerance" that allows too much domestic dissent.

These policies were, in fact, already being implemented. In 1949, US espionage in Eastern Europe had been turned over to a network run by Reinhard Gehlen, who had headed Nazi military intelligence on the Eastern Front. This network was one part of the US-Nazi alliance that quickly absorbed many of the worst criminals, extending to operations in Latin America and elsewhere.

These operations included a "secret army" under US-Nazi auspices that sought to provide agents and military supplies to armies that had been established by Hitler and which were still operating inside the Soviet Union and Eastern Europe through the early 1950s. (This is known in the US but considered insignificant—although it might raise a few eyebrows if the tables were turned and we discovered that, say, the Soviet Union had dropped agents and supplies to armies established by Hitler that were operating in the Rockies.)

The liberal extreme

NSC 68 is the hard-line extreme, and remember: the policies weren't just theoretical—many of them were actually being implemented. Now let's turn to the other extreme, to the doves. The leading dove was undoubtedly George Kennan, who headed the State Department planning staff until 1950, when he was replaced by Nitze— Kennan's office, incidentally, was responsible for the Gehlen network.

Kennan was one of the most intelligent and lucid of US planners, and a major figure in shaping the postwar world. His writings are an extremely interesting illustration of the dovish position. One document to look at if you want to understand your country is Policy Planning Study 23, written by Kennan for the State Department planning staff in 1948. Here's some of what it says:

> we have about 50% of the world's wealth, but only 6.3% of its population....In this situation, we cannot fail to be the object of envy and resentment. Our real task in the coming period is to devise a pattern of relationships which will permit us to maintain this position of disparity....To do so, we will have to dispense with all sentimentality and day-dreaming; and our attention will have to be concentrated

everywhere on our immediate national objectives....We should cease to talk about vague and...unreal objectives such as human rights, the raising of the living standards, and democratization. The day is not far off when we are going to have to deal in straight power concepts. The less we are then hampered by idealistic slogans, the better.

PPS 23 was, of course, a top-secret document. To pacify the public, it was necessary to trumpet the "idealistic slogans" (as is still being done constantly), but here planners were talking to one another.

Along the same lines, in a briefing for US ambassadors to Latin American countries in 1950, Kennan observed that a major concern of US foreign policy must be "the protection of our [i.e. Latin America's] raw materials." We must therefore combat a dangerous heresy which, US intelligence reported, was spreading through Latin America: "the idea that the government has direct responsibility for the welfare of the people."

US planners call that idea *Communism*, whatever the actual political views of the people advocating it. They can be Church-based self-help groups or whatever, but if they support this heresy, they're Communists.

This point is also made clear in the public record. For example, a high-level study group in 1955 stated that the essential threat of the Communist powers (the real meaning of the term *Communism* in practice) is their refusal to fulfill their service role—that is, "to complement the industrial economies of the West."

Kennan went on to explain the means we have to use against our enemies who fall prey to this heresy:

> The final answer might be an unpleasant one, but...we should not hesitate before police repression by the local government. This is not shameful since the Communists are essentially traitors....It is better to have a strong regime in power than a liberal government if it is indulgent and relaxed and penetrated by Communists.

Policies like these didn't begin with postwar liberals like Kennan. As Woodrow Wilson's Secretary of State had already pointed out 30 years earlier, the operative meaning of the Monroe Doctrine is that "the United States considers its own interests. The integrity of other American nations is an incident, not an end." Wilson, the great apostle of self-determination, agreed that the argument was "unanswerable," though it would be "impolitic" to present it publicly.

Wilson also acted on this thinking by, among other things, invading Haiti and the Dominican Republic, where his warriors murdered and destroyed, demolished the political system, left US corporations firmly in control, and set the stage for brutal and corrupt dictatorships.

The "Grand Area"

During World War II, study groups of the State Department and Council on Foreign Relations developed plans for the postwar world in terms of what they called the "Grand Area," which was to be subordinated to the needs of the American economy.

The Grand Area was to include the Western Hemisphere, Western Europe, the Far East, the former British Empire (which was being dismantled), the incomparable energy resources of the Middle East (which were then passing into American hands as we pushed out our rivals France and Britain), the rest of the Third World and, if possible, the entire globe. These plans were implemented, as opportunities allowed.

Every part of the new world order was assigned a specific function. The industrial countries were to be guided by the "great workshops," Germany and Japan, who had demonstrated their prowess during the war (and now would be working under US supervision).

The Third World was to "fulfill its major function as a source of raw materials and a market" for the industrial capitalist societies, as a 1949 State Department memo put it. It was to be "exploited" (in Kennan's words) for the reconstruction of Europe and Japan. (The references are to Southeast Asia and Africa, but the points are general.)

Kennan even suggested that Europe might get a psychological lift from the project of "exploiting" Africa. Naturally, no one suggested that Africa should exploit Europe for its reconstruction, perhaps also improving its state of mind. These declassified documents are read only by scholars, who apparently find nothing odd or jarring in all this.

The Vietnam War emerged from the need to ensure this service role. Vietnamese nationalists didn't want to accept it, so they had to be smashed. The threat wasn't that they were going to conquer anyone, but that they might set a dangerous example of national independence that would inspire other nations in the region.

The US government had two major roles to play. The first was to secure the far-flung domains of the Grand Area. That required a very intimidating posture, to ensure that no one interferes with this task—which is one reason why there's been such a drive for nuclear weapons.

The government's second role was to organize a public subsidy for high-technology industry. For various reasons, the method adopted has been military spending, in large part.

Free trade is fine for economics departments and newspaper editorials, but nobody in the corporate world or the government takes the doctrines seriously. The parts of the US economy that are able to compete internationally are primarily the state-subsidized ones: capital-intensive agriculture (*agribusiness*, as it's called), high-tech industry, pharmaceuticals, biotechnology, etc.

The same is true of other industrial societies. The US government has the public pay for research and development and provides, largely through the military, a state-guaranteed market for waste production. If something is marketable, the private sector takes it over. That system of public subsidy and private profit is what is called *free enterprise*.

Restoring the traditional order

Postwar planners like Kennan realized right off that it was going to be vital for the health of US corporations that the other Western industrial societies reconstruct from wartime damage so they could import US manufactured goods and provide investment opportunities. (I'm counting Japan as part of the West, following the South African convention of treating Japanese as "honorary whites.") But it was crucial that these societies reconstruct in a very specific way.

The traditional, right-wing order had to be restored, with business dominant, labor split and weakened, and the burden of reconstruction placed squarely on the shoulders of the working classes and the poor.

The major thing that stood in the way of this was the antifascist resistance, so we suppressed it all over the world, often installing fascists and Nazi collaborators in its place. Sometimes that required extreme violence, but other times it was done by softer measures, like subverting elections and withholding desperately needed food. (This ought to be Chapter 1 in any honest history of the postwar period, but in fact it's seldom even discussed.)

The pattern was set in 1942, when President Roosevelt installed a French Admiral, Jean Darlan, as Governor-General of all of French North Africa. Darlan was a leading Nazi collaborator and the author of the antisemitic laws promulgated by the Vichy government (the Nazis' puppet regime in France).

But far more important was the first area of Europe liberated—southern Italy, where the US, following Churchill's advice, imposed a right-wing dictatorship headed by Fascist war hero Field Marshall Badoglio and the King, Victor Emmanuel III, who was also a Fascist collaborator.

US planners recognized that the "threat" in Europe was not Soviet aggression (which serious analysts, like Dwight Eisenhower, did not anticipate) but rather the worker- and peasant-based antifascist resistance with its radical democratic ideals, and the political power and appeal of the local Communist parties.

To prevent an economic collapse that would enhance their influence, and to rebuild Western Europe's state-capitalist economies, the US instituted the Marshall Plan (under which Europe was provided with more than $12 billion in loans and grants between 1948 and 1951, funds used to purchase a third of US exports to Europe in the peak year of 1949).

In Italy, a worker- and peasant-based movement, led by the Communist party, had held down six German divisions during the war and liberated northern Italy. As US forces advanced through Italy, they dispersed this antifascist resistance and restored the basic structure of the prewar Fascist regime.

Italy has been one of the main areas of CIA subversion ever since the agency was founded. The CIA was concerned about Communists winning power legally in the crucial Italian elections of 1948. A lot of techniques were used, including restoring the Fascist police, breaking the unions and withholding food. But it wasn't clear that the Communist party could be defeated.

The very first National Security Council memorandum, NSC 1 (1948), specified a number of actions the US would take if the Communists won these elections. One planned response was armed intervention, by means of military aid for underground operations in Italy.

Some people, particularly George Kennan, advocated military action *before* the elections— he didn't want to take a chance. But others convinced him we could carry it off by subversion, which turned out to be correct.

In Greece, British troops entered after the Nazis had withdrawn. They imposed a corrupt regime that evoked renewed resistance, and Britain, in its postwar decline, was unable to maintain control. In 1947, the United States moved in, supporting a murderous war that resulted in about 160,000 deaths.

This war was complete with torture, political exile for tens of thousands of Greeks, what we called "re-education camps" for tens of thousands of others, and the destruction of unions and of any possibility of independent politics.

It placed Greece firmly in the hands of US investors and local businessmen, while much of the population had to emigrate in order to survive. The beneficiaries included Nazi collaborators, while the primary victims were the workers and the peasants of the Communist-led, anti-Nazi resistance.

Our successful defense of Greece against its own population was the model for the Vietnam

War—as Adlai Stevenson explained to the United Nations in 1964. Reagan's advisors used exactly the same model in talking about Central America, and the pattern was followed many other places.

In Japan, Washington initiated the so-called "reverse course" of 1947 that terminated early steps towards democratization taken by General MacArthur's military administration. The reverse course suppressed the unions and other democratic forces and placed the country firmly in the hands of corporate elements that had backed Japanese fascism—a system of state and private power that still endures.

When US forces entered Korea in 1945, they dispersed the local popular government, consisting primarily of antifascists who resisted the Japanese, and inaugurated a brutal repression, using Japanese fascist police and Koreans who had collaborated with them during the Japanese occupation. About 100,000 people were murdered in South Korea prior to what we call the Korean War, including 30–40,000 killed during the suppression of a peasant revolt in one small region, Cheju Island.

A fascist coup in Colombia, inspired by Franco's Spain, brought little protest from the US government; neither did a military coup in Venezuela, nor the restoration of an admirer of fascism in Panama. But the first democratic government in the history of Guatemala, which modeled itself on Roosevelt's New Deal, elicited bitter US antagonism.

In 1954, the CIA engineered a coup that turned Guatemala into a hell on earth. It's been kept that way ever since, with regular US intervention and support, particularly under Kennedy and Johnson.

One aspect of suppressing the antifascist resistance was the recruitment of war criminals like Klaus Barbie, an SS officer who had been the Gestapo chief of Lyon, France. There he earned his nickname: the Butcher of Lyon. Although he was responsible for many hideous crimes, the US Army put him in charge of spying on the French.

When Barbie was finally brought back to France in 1982 to be tried as a war criminal, his use as an agent was explained by Colonel (ret.) Eugene Kolb of the US Army Counterintelligence Corps: Barbie's "skills were badly needed....His activities had been directed against the underground French Communist party and the resistance," who were now targeted for repression by the American liberators.

Since the United States was picking up where the Nazis had left off, it made perfect sense to employ specialists in antiresistance activities. Later on, when it became difficult or impossible to protect these useful folks in Europe, many of them (including Barbie) were spirited off to the United States or to Latin America, often with the help of the Vatican and fascist priests.

There they became military advisers to US-supported police states that were modeled, often quite openly, on the Third Reich. They also became drug dealers, weapons merchants, terrorists and educators—teaching Latin American peasants torture techniques devised by the Gestapo. Some of the Nazis' students ended up in Central America, thus establishing a direct link between the death camps and the death squads—all thanks to the postwar alliance between the US and the SS.

Our commitment to democracy

In one high-level document after another, US planners stated their view that the primary threat to the new US-led world order was Third World nationalism—sometimes called *ultranationalism:* "nationalistic regimes" that are responsive to "popular demand for immediate improvement in the low living standards of the masses" and production for domestic needs.

The planners' basic goals, repeated over and over again, were to prevent such "ultranationalist" regimes from ever taking power—or if, by some fluke, they did take power, to remove them and to install governments that favor private investment of domestic and foreign capital, production for export and the right to bring profits out of the country. (These goals are never challenged in the secret documents. If you're a US policy planner, they're sort of like the air you breathe.)

Opposition to democracy and social reform is never popular in the victim country. You can't get many of the people living there excited about it, except a small group connected with US businesses who are going to profit from it.

The United States expects to rely on force, and makes alliances with the military—"the least anti-American of any political group in Latin

America," as the Kennedy planners put it—so they can be relied on to crush any indigenous popular groups that get out of hand.

The US has been willing to tolerate social reform—as in Costa Rica, for example—*only* when the rights of labor are suppressed and the climate for foreign investment is preserved. Because the Costa Rican government has always respected these two crucial imperatives, it's been allowed to play around with its reforms.

Another problem that's pointed to over and over again in these secret documents is the excessive liberalism of Third World countries. (That was particularly a problem in Latin America, where the governments weren't sufficiently committed to thought control and restrictions on travel, and where the legal systems were so deficient that they required evidence for the prosecution of crimes.)

This is a constant lament right through the Kennedy period (after that, the documentary record hasn't yet been declassified). The Kennedy liberals were adamant about the need to overcome democratic excesses that permitted "subversion"—by which, of course, they meant people thinking the wrong ideas.

The United States was not, however, lacking in compassion for the poor. For example, in the mid-1950s, our ambassador to Costa Rica recommended that the United Fruit Company, which basically ran Costa Rica, introduce "a few relatively simple and superficial human-interest frills for the workers that may have a large psychological effect."

Secretary of State John Foster Dulles agreed, telling President Eisenhower that to keep Latin Americans in line, "you have to pat them a little bit and make them think that you are fond of them."

Given all that, US policies in the Third World are easy to understand. We've consistently opposed democracy if its results can't be controlled. The problem with real democracies is that they're likely to fall prey to the heresy that governments should respond to the needs of their own population, instead of those of US investors.

A study of the inter-American system published by the Royal Institute of International Affairs in London concluded that, while the US pays lip service to democracy, the real commitment is to "private, capitalist enterprise." When the rights of investors are threatened, democracy has to go; if these rights are safeguarded, killers and torturers will do just fine.

Parliamentary governments were barred or overthrown, with US support and sometimes direct intervention, in Iran in 1953, in Guatemala in 1954 (and in 1963, when Kennedy backed a military coup to prevent the threat of return to democracy), in the Dominican Republic in 1963 and 1965, in Brazil in 1964, in Chile in 1973 and often elsewhere. Our policies have been very much the same in El Salvador and in many other places across the globe.

The methods are not very pretty. What the US-run contra forces did in Nicaragua, or what our terrorist proxies do in El Salvador or Guatemala, isn't only ordinary killing. A major element is brutal, sadistic torture—beating infants against rocks, hanging women by their feet with their breasts cut off and the skin of their face peeled back so that they'll bleed to death, chopping people's heads off and putting them on stakes. The point is to crush independent nationalism and popular forces that might bring about meaningful democracy.

The threat of a good example

No country is exempt from this treatment, no matter how unimportant. In fact, it's the weakest, poorest countries that often arouse the greatest hysteria.

Take Laos in the 1960s, probably the poorest country in the world. Most of the people who lived there didn't even know there was such a thing as Laos; they just knew they had a little village and there was another little village nearby.

But as soon as a very low-level social revolution began to develop there, Washington subjected Laos to a murderous "secret bombing," virtually wiping out large settled areas in operations that, it was conceded, had nothing to do with the war the US was waging in South Vietnam.

Grenada has a hundred thousand people who produce a little nutmeg, and you could hardly find it on a map. But when Grenada began to undergo a mild social revolution, Washington quickly moved to destroy the threat.

From the Bolshevik Revolution of 1917 till the collapse of the Communist governments in Eastern Europe in the late 1980s, it was possible to justify every US attack as a defense against the Soviet threat. So when the United States invaded Grenada in 1983, the chairman of the Joint Chiefs of Staff explained that, in the event of a Soviet attack on Western Europe, a hostile Grenada could interdict oil supplies from the Caribbean to Western Europe and we wouldn't be able to defend our beleaguered allies. Now this sounds comical, but that kind of story helps mobilize public support for aggression, terror and subversion.

The attack against Nicaragua was justified by the claim that if we don't stop "them" there, they'll be pouring across the border at Harlingen, Texas—just two days' drive away. (For educated people, there were more sophisticated variants, just about as plausible.)

As far as American business is concerned, Nicaragua could disappear and nobody would notice. The same is true of El Salvador. But both have been subjected to murderous assaults by the US, at a cost of hundreds of thousands of lives and many billions of dollars.

There's a reason for that. The weaker and poorer a country is, the more dangerous it is *as an example.* If a tiny, poor country like Grenada can succeed in bringing about a better life for its people, some other place that has more resources will ask, "why not us?"

This was even true in Indochina, which is pretty big and has some significant resources. Although Eisenhower and his advisers ranted a lot about the rice and tin and rubber, the real fear was that if the people of Indochina achieved independence and justice, the people of Thailand would emulate it, and if that worked, they'd try it in Malaya, and pretty soon Indonesia would pursue an independent path, and by then a significant area of the Grand Area would have been lost.

If you want a global system that's subordinated to the needs of US investors, you can't let pieces of it wander off. It's striking how clearly this is stated in the documentary record—even in the public record at times. Take Chile under Allende.

Chile is a fairly big place, with a lot of natural resources, but again, the United States wasn't going to collapse if Chile became independent. Why were we so concerned about it? According to Kissinger, Chile was a "virus" that would "infect" the region with effects all the way to Italy.

Despite 40 years of CIA subversion, Italy still has a labor movement. Seeing a social democratic government succeed in Chile would send the wrong message to Italian voters. Suppose they get funny ideas about taking control of their own country and revive the workers' movements the CIA undermined in the 1940s?

US planners from Secretary of State Dean Acheson in the late 1940s to the present have warned that "one rotten apple can spoil the barrel." The danger is that the "rot"—social and economic development—may spread.

This "rotten apple theory" is called the domino theory for public consumption. The version used to frighten the public has Ho Chi Minh getting in a canoe and landing in California, and so on.

Maybe some US leaders believe this nonsense—it's possible—but rational planners certainly don't. They understand that the real threat is the "good example."

Sometimes the point is explained with great clarity. When the US was planning to overthrow Guatemalan democracy in 1954, a State Department official pointed out that "Guatemala has become an increasing threat to the stability of Honduras and El Salvador. Its agrarian reform is a powerful propaganda weapon; its broad social program of aiding the workers and peasants in a victorious struggle against the upper classes and large foreign enterprises has a strong appeal to the populations of Central American neighbors where similar conditions prevail."

In other words, what the US wants is "stability," meaning security for the "upper classes and large foreign enterprises." If that can be achieved with formal democratic devices, OK. If not, the "threat to stability" posed by a good example has to be destroyed before the virus infects others.

That's why even the tiniest speck poses such a threat, and may have to be crushed.

The three-sided world

From the early 1970s, the world has been drifting into what's called *tripolarism* or *trilateralism*—three major economic blocs that compete with each other. The first is a yen-based bloc with Japan as its center and the former Japanese colonies on the periphery.

Back in the thirties and forties, Japan called that The Greater East Asia Co-Prosperity

Sphere. The conflict with the US arose from Japan's attempt to exercise the same kind of control there that the Western powers exercised in their own spheres. But after the war, we reconstructed the region for them. We then had no problem with Japan exploiting it—they just had to do it under our overarching power.

There's a lot of nonsense written about how the fact that Japan became a major competitor proves how honorable we are and how we built up our enemies. The actual policy options, however, were narrower. One was to restore Japan's empire, but now all under our control (this was the policy that was followed).

The other option was to keep out of the region and allow Japan and the rest of Asia to follow their independent paths, excluded from the Grand Area of US control. That was unthinkable.

Furthermore, after WW II, Japan was not regarded as a possible competitor, even in the remote future. It was assumed that maybe somewhere down the road Japan would be able to produce knickknacks, but nothing beyond that. (There was a strong element of racism in this.) Japan recovered in large part because of the Korean War and then the Vietnam War, which stimulated Japanese production and brought Japan huge profits.

A few of the early postwar planners were more far-sighted, George Kennan among them. He proposed that the United States encourage Japan to industrialize, but with one limit: the US would control Japanese oil imports. Kennan said this would allow us "veto power" over

Japan in case it ever got out of line. The US followed this advice, keeping control over Japan's oil supplies and refineries. As late as the early 1970s, Japan still controlled only about 10% of its own oil supplies.

That's one of the main reasons the United States has been so interested in Middle Eastern oil. We didn't need the oil for ourselves; until 1968, North America led world oil production. But we do want to keep our hands on this lever of world power, and make sure that the profits flow primarily to the US and Britain.

That's one reason why we have maintained military bases in the Philippines. They're part of a global intervention system aimed at the Middle East to make sure indigenous forces there don't succumb to "ultranationalism."

The second major competitive bloc is based in Europe and is dominated by Germany. It's taking a big step forward with the consolidation of the European Common Market. Europe has a larger economy than the United States, a larger population and a better educated one.

If it ever gets its act together and becomes an integrated power, the United States could become a second-class power. This is even more likely as German-led Europe takes the lead in restoring Eastern Europe to its traditional role as an economic colony, basically part of the Third World.

The third bloc is the US-dominated, dollar-based one. It was recently extended to incorporate Canada, our major trading partner, and will soon include Mexico and other parts of the hemisphere, through "free trade agreements" designed primarily for the interests of US investors and their associates.

We've always assumed that Latin America belongs to us by right. As Henry Stimson (Secretary of War under FDR and Taft, Secretary of State under Hoover), once put it, it's "our little region over here, which never has bothered anybody." Securing the dollar-based bloc means that the drive to thwart independent development in Central America and the Caribbean will continue.

Unless you understand our struggles against our industrial rivals and the Third World, US foreign policy appears to be a series of random errors, inconsistencies and confusions. Actually, our leaders have succeeded rather well at their assigned chores, within the limits of feasibility.

Devastation abroad

Our Good Neighbor policy

How well have the precepts put forth by George Kennan been followed? How thoroughly have we put aside all concern for "vague and unreal objectives such as human rights, the raising of the living standards, and democratization"? I've already discussed our "commitment to democracy," but what about the other two issues?

Let's focus on Latin America, and begin by looking at human rights. A study by Lars Schoultz, the leading academic specialist on human rights there, shows that "US aid has tended to flow disproportionately to Latin American governments which torture their citizens." It has nothing to do with how much a country *needs* aid, only with its willingness to serve the interests of wealth and privilege.

Broader studies by economist Edward Herman reveal a close correlation worldwide between torture and US aid, and also provide the explanation: both correlate independently with improving the climate for business operations. In comparison with that guiding moral principle, such matters as torture and butchery pale into insignificance.

How about raising living standards? That was supposedly addressed by President Kennedy's Alliance for Progress, but the kind of development imposed was oriented mostly towards the needs of US investors. It entrenched and extended the existing system in which Latin Americans are made to produce crops for export and to cut back on subsistence crops like corn and beans grown for local consumption. Under Alliance programs, for example, beef production increased while beef consumption declined.

This agro-export model of development usually produces an "economic miracle" where GNP goes up while much of the population starves. When you pursue such policies, popular opposition inevitably develops, which you then suppress with terror and torture.

(The use of terror is deeply ingrained in our character. Back in 1818, John Quincy Adams hailed the "salutary efficacy" of terror in dealing with "mingled hordes of lawless Indians and negroes." He wrote that to justify Andrew Jackson's rampages in Florida which virtually annihilated the native population and left the Spanish province under US control, much impressing Thomas Jefferson and others with his wisdom.)

The first step is to use the police. They're critical because they can detect discontent early and eliminate it before "major surgery" (as the planning documents call it) is necessary. If major surgery does become necessary, we rely on the army. When we can no longer control the army of a Latin American country—particularly one in the Caribbean-Central American region— it's time to overthrow the government.

Countries that have attempted to reverse the pattern, such as Guatemala under the democratic capitalist governments of Arévalo and Arbenz, or the Dominican Republic under the democratic capitalist regime of Bosch, became the target of US hostility and violence.

The second step is to use the military. The US has always tried to establish relations with the military in foreign countries, because that's one of the ways to overthrow a government that has gotten out of hand. That's how the basis was laid for military coups in Chile in 1973 and in Indonesia in 1965.

Before the coups, we were very hostile to the Chilean and Indonesian governments, but we continued to send them arms. Keep good relations with the right officers and they overthrow the government *for* you. The same reasoning motivated the flow of US arms to Iran via Israel from the early 1980s, according to the high Israeli officials involved, facts well-known by 1982, long before there were any hostages.

During the Kennedy administration, the mission of the US-dominated Latin American military was shifted from "hemispheric defense" to "internal security" (which basically means war against your own population). That fateful decision led to "direct [US] complicity" in "the methods of Heinrich Himmler's extermination squads," in the retrospective judgment of Charles Maechling, who was in charge of counterinsurgency planning from 1961–66.

The Kennedy Administration prepared the way for the 1964 military coup in Brazil, helping to destroy Brazilian democracy, which was becoming too independent. The US gave enthusiastic support to the coup, while its military leaders instituted a neo-Nazi-style national security state with torture, repression, etc. That inspired a rash of similar developments in Argentina, Chile and all over the hemisphere, from the mid-sixties to the eighties—an extremely bloody period.

(I think, legally speaking, there's a very solid case for impeaching every American president since the Second World War. They've all been either outright war criminals or involved in serious war crimes.)

The military typically proceeds to create an economic disaster, often following the prescriptions of US advisers, and then decides to hand the problem over to civilians to administer. Overt military control is no longer necessary as new devices become available—for example, controls exercised through the International Monetary Fund (which, like the World Bank, lends Third World nations funds largely provided by the industrial powers).

In return for its loans, the IMF imposes "liberalization": an economy open to foreign penetration and control, sharp cutbacks in services to the general population, etc. These measures place power even more firmly in the hands of the wealthy classes and foreign investors ("stability") and reinforce the classic two-tiered societies of the Third World—the super-rich (and a relatively well-off professional class that serves them) and an enormous mass of impoverished, suffering people.

The indebtedness and economic chaos left by the military pretty much ensures that the IMF rules will be followed—unless popular forces attempt to enter the political arena, in which case the military may have to reinstate "stability."

Brazil is an instructive case. It is so well endowed with natural resources that it ought to be one of the richest countries in the world, and it also has high industrial development. But, thanks in good measure to the 1964 coup and the highly praised "economic miracle" that followed (not to speak of the torture, murder and other devices of "population control"), the situation for many Brazilians is now probably on a par with Ethiopia—vastly worse than in Eastern Europe, for example.

The Ministry of Education reports that over a third of the education budget goes to school meals, because most of the students in public schools either eat at school or not at all.

According to *South* magazine (a business magazine reporting on the Third World), Brazil has a higher infant mortality rate than Sri Lanka. A third of the population lives below the poverty line and "seven million abandoned children beg, steal and sniff glue on the streets. For scores of millions, home is a shack in a slum...or increasingly, a patch of ground under a bridge."

That's Brazil, one of the naturally richest countries in the world.

The situation is similar throughout Latin America. Just in Central America, the number of people murdered by US-backed forces since the late 1970s comes to something like 200,000, as popular movements that sought democracy and social reform were decimated. These achievements qualify the US as an "inspiration for the triumph of democracy in our time," in the admiring words of the liberal *New Republic.* Tom Wolfe tells us the 1980s were "one of the great golden moments that humanity has ever experienced." As Stalin used to say, we're "dizzy with success."

The crucifixion of El Salvador

For many years, repression, torture and murder were carried on in El Salvador by dictators installed and supported by our government, a matter of no interest here. The story was virtually never covered. By the late 1970s, however, the US government began to be concerned about a couple of things.

One was that Somoza, the dictator of Nicaragua, was losing control. The US was losing a major base for its exercise of force in the region. A second danger was even more threatening. In El Salvador in the 1970s, there was a growth of what were called "popular organizations"—peasant associations, cooperatives, unions, Church-based Bible study groups that evolved into self-help groups, etc. That raised the threat of democracy.

In February 1980, the Archbishop of El Salvador, Oscar Romero, sent a letter to President Carter in which he begged him not to send military aid to the junta that ran the country. He said such aid would be used to "sharpen injustice and repression against the people's organizations" which were struggling "for respect for their most basic human rights" (hardly news to Washington, needless to say).

A few weeks later, Archbishop Romero was assassinated while saying a mass. The neo-Nazi

Roberto d'Aubuisson is generally assumed to be responsible for this assassination (among countless other atrocities). D'Aubuisson was "leader-for-life" of the ARENA party, which now governs El Salvador; members of the party, like current Salvadoran president Alfredo Cristiani, had to take a blood oath of loyalty to him.

Thousands of peasants and urban poor took part in a commemorative mass a decade later, along with many foreign bishops, but the US was notable by its absence. The Salvadoran Church formally proposed Romero for sainthood.

All of this passed with scarcely a mention in the country that funded and trained Romero's assassins. The *New York Times*, the "newspaper of record," published no editorial on the assassination when it occurred or in the years that followed, and no editorial or news report on the commemoration.

On March 7, 1980, two weeks before the assassination, a state of siege had been instituted in El Salvador, and the war against the population began in force (with continued US support and involvement). The first major attack was a big massacre at the Rio Sumpul, a coordinated military operation of the Honduran and Salvadoran armies in which at least 600 people were butchered. Infants were cut to pieces with machetes, and women were tortured and drowned. Pieces of bodies were found in the river for days afterwards. There were church observers, so the information came out immediately, but the mainstream US media didn't think it was worth reporting.

Peasants were the main victims of this war, along with labor organizers, students, priests or anyone suspected of working for the interests of the people. In Carter's last year, 1980, the death toll reached about 10,000, rising to about 13,000 for 1981 as the Reaganites took command.

In October 1980, the new archbishop condemned the "war of extermination and genocide against a defenseless civilian population" waged by the security forces. Two months later they were hailed for their "valiant service alongside the people against subversion" by the favorite US "moderate," José Napoleón Duarte, as he was appointed civilian president of the junta.

The role of the "moderate" Duarte was to provide a fig leaf for the military rulers and ensure them a continuing flow of US funding after the armed forces had raped and murdered four churchwomen from the US. That had aroused some protest here; slaughtering Salvadorans is one thing, but raping and killing American nuns is a definite PR mistake. The media evaded and downplayed the story, following the lead of the Carter Administration and its investigative commission.

The incoming Reaganites went much further, seeking to justify the atrocity, notably Secretary of State Alexander Haig and UN Ambassador Jeane Kirkpatrick. But it was still deemed worthwhile to have a show trial a few years later, while exculpating the murderous junta—and, of course, the paymaster.

The independent newspapers in El Salvador, which might have reported these atrocities, had been destroyed. Although they were mainstream and pro-business, they were still too undisciplined for the military's taste. The problem was taken care of in 1980-81, when the editor of one was murdered by the security forces; the other fled into exile. As usual, these events were considered too insignificant to merit more than a few words in US newspapers.

In November 1989, six Jesuit priests, their cook and her daughter, were murdered by the army. That same week, at least 28 other Salvadoran civilians were murdered, including the head of a major union, the leader of the organization of university women, nine members of an Indian farming cooperative and ten university students.

The news wires carried a story by AP correspondent Douglas Grant Mine, reporting how soldiers had entered a working-class neighborhood in the capital city of San Salvador, captured six men, added a 14-year-old boy for good measure, then lined them all up against a wall and shot them. They "were not priests or human rights campaigners," Mine wrote, "so their deaths have gone largely unnoticed"—as did his story.

The Jesuits were murdered by the Atlacatl Battalion, an elite unit created, trained and equipped by the United States. It was formed in March 1981, when fifteen specialists in counterinsurgency were sent to El Salvador from the US Army School of Special Forces. From the start, the Battalion was engaged in mass murder. A US trainer described its soldiers as "particularly ferocious....We've always had a hard time getting [them] to take prisoners instead of ears."

In December 1981, the Battalion took part in an operation in which over a thousand civilians were killed in an orgy of murder, rape and burning. Later it was involved in the bombing of villages and murder of hundreds of civilians by shooting, drowning and other methods. The vast majority of victims were women, children and the elderly.

The Atlacatl Battalion was being trained by US Special Forces shortly before murdering the Jesuits. This has been a pattern throughout the Battalion's existence—some of its worst massacres have occurred when it was fresh from US training.

In the "fledgling democracy" that was El Salvador, teenagers as young as 13 were scooped up in sweeps of slums and refugee camps and forced to become soldiers. They were indoctrinated with rituals adopted from the Nazi SS, including brutalization and rape, to prepare them for killings that often have sexual and satanic overtones.

The nature of Salvadoran army training was described by a deserter who received political asylum in Texas in 1990, despite the State Department's request that he be sent back to El Salvador. (His name was withheld by the court to protect him from Salvadoran death squads.)

According to this deserter, draftees were made to kill dogs and vultures by biting their throats and twisting off their heads, and had to watch as soldiers tortured and killed suspected dissidents—tearing out their fingernails, cutting off their heads, chopping their bodies to pieces and playing with the dismembered arms for fun.

In another case, an admitted member of a Salvadoran death squad associated with the Atlacatl Battalion, César Vielman Joya Martínez, detailed the involvement of US advisers and the Salvadoran government in death-squad activity. The Bush administration has made every effort to silence him and ship him back to probable death in El Salvador, despite the pleas of human rights organizations and requests from Congress that his testimony be heard. (The treatment of the main witness to the assassination of the Jesuits was similar.)

The results of Salvadoran military training are graphically described in the Jesuit journal *America* by Daniel Santiago, a Catholic priest working in El Salvador. He tells of a peasant woman who returned home one day to find her three children, her mother and her sister sitting around a table, each with its own decapitated head placed carefully on the table in front of the body, the hands arranged on top "as if each body was stroking its own head."

The assassins, from the Salvadoran National Guard, had found it hard to keep the head of an 18-month-old baby in place, so they nailed the hands onto it. A large plastic bowl filled with blood was tastefully displayed in the center of the table.

According to Rev. Santiago, macabre scenes of this kind aren't uncommon.

People are not just killed by death squads in El Salvador—they are decapitated and then their heads are placed on pikes and used to dot the landscape. Men are not just disemboweled by the

Salvadoran Treasury Police; their severed genitalia are stuffed into their mouths. Salvadoran women are not just raped by the National Guard; their wombs are cut from their bodies and used to cover their faces. It is not enough to kill children; they are dragged over barbed wire until the flesh falls from their bones, while parents are forced to watch.

Rev. Santiago goes on to point out that violence of this sort greatly increased when the Church began forming peasant associations and self-help groups in an attempt to organize the poor.

By and large, our approach in El Salvador has been successful. The popular organizations have been decimated, just as Archbishop Romero predicted. Tens of thousands have been slaughtered and more than a million have become refugees. This is one of the most sordid episodes in US history—and it's got a lot of competition.

Teaching Nicaragua a lesson

It wasn't just El Salvador that was ignored by the mainstream US media during the 1970s. In the ten years prior to the overthrow of the Nicaraguan dictator Anastasio Somoza in 1979, US television—all networks—devoted exactly *one hour* to Nicaragua, and that was entirely on the Managua earthquake of 1972.

From 1960 through 1978, the *New York Times* had three editorials on Nicaragua. It's not that nothing was happening there—it's just that whatever was happening was unremarkable. Nicaragua was of no concern at all, as long as Somoza's tyrannical rule wasn't challenged.

When his rule *was* challenged, by the Sandinistas in the late 1970s, the US first tried to institute what was called "Somocismo [Somoza-ism] without Somoza"—that is, the whole corrupt system intact, but with somebody else at the top. That didn't work, so President Carter tried to maintain Somoza's National Guard as a base for US power.

The National Guard had always been remarkably brutal and sadistic. By June 1979, it was carrying out massive atrocities in the war against the Sandinistas, bombing residential neighborhoods in Managua, killing tens of thousands of people. At that point, the US ambassador sent a cable to the White House saying it would be "ill-advised" to tell the Guard to call off the bombing, because that might interfere with the policy of keeping them in power and the Sandinistas out.

Our ambassador to the Organization of American States also spoke in favor of "Somocismo without Somoza," but the OAS rejected the suggestion flat out. A few days later, Somoza flew off to Miami with what was left of the Nicaraguan national treasury, and the Guard collapsed.

The Carter administration flew Guard commanders out of the country in planes with Red Cross markings (a war crime), and began to reconstitute the Guard on Nicaragua's borders. They also used Argentina as a proxy. (At that time, Argentina was under the rule of neo-Nazi generals, but they took a little time off from torturing and murdering their own population to help reestablish the Guard—soon to be renamed the *contras*, or "freedom fighters.")

Reagan used them to launch a large-scale terrorist war against Nicaragua, combined with economic warfare that was even more lethal. We also intimidated other countries so they wouldn't send aid either.

And yet, despite astronomical levels of military support, the United States failed to create a viable military force in Nicaragua. That's quite remarkable, if you think about it. No real guerillas anywhere in the world have ever had resources even remotely like what the United States gave the contras. You could probably start a guerilla insurgency in mountain regions of the US with comparable funding.

Why did the US go to such lengths in Nicaragua? The international development organization Oxfam explained the real reasons, stating that, from its experience of working in 76 developing countries, "Nicaragua was...exceptional in the strength of that government's commitment...to improving the condition of the people and encouraging their active participation in the development process."

Of the four Central American countries where Oxfam had a significant presence (El Salvador, Guatemala, Honduras and Nicaragua), only in Nicaragua was there a substantial effort to address inequities in land ownership and to extend health, educational and agricultural services to poor peasant families.

Other agencies told a similar story. In the early 1980s, the World Bank called its projects "extraordinarily successful in Nicaragua in some sectors, better than anywhere else in the world."

In 1983, The Inter-American Development Bank concluded that "Nicaragua has made noteworthy progress in the social sector, which is laying the basis for long-term socio-economic development."

The success of the Sandinista reforms terrified US planners. They were aware that—as José Figueres, the father of Costa Rican democracy, put it—"for the first time, Nicaragua has a government that cares for its people." (Although Figueres was the leading democratic figure in Central America for forty years, his unacceptable insights into the real world were completely censored from the US media.)

The hatred that was elicited by the Sandinistas for trying to direct resources to the poor (and even succeeding at it) was truly wondrous to behold. Just about all US policymakers shared it, and it reached virtual frenzy.

Back in 1981, a State Department insider boasted that we would "turn Nicaragua into the Albania of Central America"—that is, poor, isolated and politically radical—so that the Sandinista dream of creating a new, more exemplary political model for Latin America would be in ruins.

George Shultz called the Sandinistas a "cancer, right here on our land mass," that has to be destroyed. At the other end of the political spectrum, leading Senate liberal Alan Cranston said that if it turned out not to be possible to destroy the Sandinistas, then we'd just have to let them "fester in [their] own juices."

So the US launched a three-fold attack against Nicaragua. First, we exerted extreme pressure to compel the World Bank and Inter-American Development Bank to terminate all projects and assistance.

Second, we launched the contra war along with an illegal economic war to terminate what Oxfam rightly called "the threat of a good example." The contras' vicious terrorist attacks against "soft targets" under US orders did help, along with the boycott, to end any hope of economic development and social reform. US terror ensured that Nicaragua couldn't demobilize its army and divert its pitifully poor and limited resources to reconstructing the ruins that were left by the US-backed dictators and Reaganite crimes.

One of the most respected Central America correspondents, Julia Preston (who was then working for the *Boston Globe*), reported that "Administration officials said they are content to see the contras debilitate the Sandinistas by forcing them to divert scarce resources toward the war and away from social programs." That's crucial, since the social programs were at the heart of the good example that might have infected other countries in the region and eroded the American system of exploitation and robbery.

We even refused to send disaster relief. After the 1972 earthquake, the US sent an enormous amount of aid to Nicaragua, most of which was stolen by our buddy Somoza. In October 1988, an even worse natural disaster struck Nicaragua—Hurricane Joan. We didn't send a penny for that, because if we had, it would probably have gotten to the people, not just into the pockets of some rich thug. We also pressured our allies to send very little aid.

This devastating hurricane, with its welcome prospects of mass starvation and long-term ecological damage, reinforced our efforts. We wanted Nicaraguans to starve so we could accuse the Sandinistas of economic mismanagement. Because they weren't under our control, Nicaraguans had to suffer and die.

Third, we used diplomatic fakery to crush Nicaragua. As Tony Avirgan wrote in the Costa Rican journal *Mesoamerica*, "the Sandinistas fell for a scam perpetrated by Costa Rican president Oscar Arias and the other Central American Presidents, which cost them the February [1990] elections."

For Nicaragua, the peace plan of August 1987 was a good deal, Avrigan wrote: they would move the scheduled national elections forward by a few months and allow international observation, as they had in 1984, "in exchange for having the *contras* demobilized and the war brought to an end...." The Nicaraguan government did what it was required to do under the peace plan, but no one else paid the slightest attention to it.

Arias, the White House and Congress never had the slightest intention of implementing any aspect of the plan. The US virtually tripled CIA supply flights to the contras. Within a couple of months the peace plan was totally dead.

As the election campaign opened, the US made it clear that the embargo that was strangling the country and the contra terror would continue if the Sandinistas won the election.

You have to be some kind of Nazi or unreconstructed Stalinist to regard an election conducted under such conditions as free and fair—and south of the border, few succumbed to such delusions.

If anything like that were ever done by our *enemies*...I leave the media reaction to your imagination. The amazing part of it was that the Sandinistas still got 40% of the vote, while *New York Times* headlines proclaimed that Americans were "United in Joy" over this "Victory for US Fair Play."

US achievements in Central America in the past fifteen years are a major tragedy, not just because of the appalling human cost, but because a decade ago there were prospects for real progress towards meaningful democracy and meeting human needs, with early successes in El Salvador, Guatemala and Nicaragua.

These efforts might have worked and might have taught useful lessons to others plagued with similar problems—which, of course, was exactly what US planners feared. The threat has been successfully aborted, perhaps forever.

Making Guatemala a killing field

There was one place in Central America that did get some US media coverage before the Sandinista revolution, and that was Guatemala. In 1944, a revolution there overthrew a vicious tyrant, leading to the establishment of a democratic government that basically modeled itself on Roosevelt's New Deal. In the ten-year democratic interlude that followed, there were the beginnings of successful independent economic development.

That caused virtual hysteria in Washington. Eisenhower and Dulles warned that the "self-defense and self-preservation" of the United States was at stake unless the virus was exterminated. US intelligence reports were very candid about the dangers posed by capitalist democracy in Guatemala.

A CIA memorandum of 1952 described the situation in Guatemala as "adverse to US interests" because of the "Communist influence... based on militant advocacy of social reforms and nationalistic policies." The memo warned that Guatemala "has recently stepped-up substantially its support of Communist and anti-American activities in other Central American countries." One prime example cited was an alleged gift of $300,000 to José Figueres.

As mentioned above, José Figueres was the founder of Costa Rican democracy and a leading democratic figure in Central America. Although he cooperated enthusiastically with the CIA, had called the United States "the standard-bearer of our cause" and was regarded by the US ambassador to Costa Rica as "the best advertising agency that the United Fruit Company could find in Latin America," Figueres had an independent streak and was therefore not considered as reliable as Somoza or other gangsters in our employ.

In the political rhetoric of the United States, this made him possibly a "Communist." So if Guatemala gave him money to help him win an election, that showed Guatemala supported Communists.

Worse yet, the same CIA memorandum continued, the "radical and nationalist policies" of the democratic capitalist government, including the "persecution of foreign economic interests, especially the United Fruit Company," had gained "the support or acquiescence of almost all Guatemalans." The government was proceeding "to mobilize the hitherto politically inert peasantry" while undermining the power of large landholders.

Furthermore, the 1944 revolution had aroused "a strong national movement to free Guatemala from the military dictatorship, social backwardness, and 'economic colonialism' which had been the pattern of the past," and "inspired the loyalty and conformed to the self-interest of most politically conscious Guatemalans." Things became still worse after a successful land reform began to threaten "stability" in neighboring countries where suffering people did not fail to take notice.

In short, the situation was pretty awful. So the CIA carried out a successful coup. Guatemala was turned into the slaughterhouse it remains today, with regular US intervention whenever things threaten to get out of line.

By the late 1970s, atrocities were again mounting beyond the terrible norm, eliciting verbal protests. And yet, contrary to what many people believe, military aid to Guatemala continued at virtually the same level under the Carter "human rights" administration. Our allies have been enlisted in the cause as well—notably Israel, which is regarded as a "strategic asset" in part because of its success in guiding state terrorism.

Under Reagan, support for near-genocide in Guatemala became positively ecstatic. The most extreme of the Guatemalan Hitlers we've backed there, Rios Montt, was lauded by Reagan as a man totally dedicated to democracy. In the early 1980s, Washington's friends slaughtered tens of thousands of Guatemalans, mostly Indians in the highlands, with countless others tortured and raped. Large regions were decimated.

In 1988, a newly opened Guatemalan newspaper called *La Epoca* was blown up by government terrorists. At the time, the media here were very much exercised over the fact that the US-funded journal in Nicaragua, *La Prensa*, which was openly calling for the overthrow of the government and supporting the US-run terrorist army, had been forced to miss a couple of issues due to a shortage of newsprint. That led to a torrent of outrage and abuse, in the *Washington Post* and elsewhere, about Sandinista totalitarianism.

On the other hand, the destruction of *La Epoca* aroused no interest whatsoever and was not reported here, although it was well-known to US journalists. Naturally the US media couldn't be expected to notice that US-funded security forces had silenced the one, tiny independent voice that had tried, a few weeks earlier, to speak up in Guatemala.

A year later, a journalist from *La Epoca*, Julio Godoy, who had fled after the bombing, went back to Guatemala for a brief visit. When he returned to the US, he contrasted the situation in Central America with that in Eastern Europe. Eastern Europeans are "luckier than Central Americans," Godoy wrote, because

> while the Moscow-imposed government in Prague would degrade and humiliate reformers, the Washington-made government in Guatemala would kill them. It still does, in a virtual genocide that has taken more than 150,000 victims [in what Amnesty International calls] "a government program of political murder."

The press either conforms or, as in the case of *La Epoca*, disappears.

"One is tempted to believe," Godoy continued, "that some people in the White House worship Aztec gods—with the offering of Central American blood." And he quoted a Western European diplomat who said: "As long as the Americans don't change their attitude towards the region, there's no space here for the truth or for hope."

The invasion of Panama

Panama has been traditionally controlled by its tiny European elite, less than 10% of the population. That changed in 1968, when Omar Torrijos, a populist general, led a coup that allowed the black and mestizo [mixed-race] poor to obtain at least a share of the power under his military dictatorship.

In 1981, Torrijos was killed in a plane crash. By 1983, the effective ruler was Manuel Noriega, a criminal who had been a cohort of Torrijos and US intelligence.

The US government knew that Noriega was involved in drug trafficking since at least 1972, when the Nixon administration considered assassinating him. But he stayed on the CIA payroll. In 1983, a US Senate committee concluded that Panama was a major center for the laundering of drug funds and drug trafficking.

The US government continued to value Noriega's services. In May 1986, the Director of the Drug Enforcement Agency praised Noriega for his "vigorous anti-drug trafficking policy." A year later, the Director "welcomed our close association" with Noriega, while Attorney-General Edwin Meese stopped a US Justice Department investigation of Noriega's criminal activities. In August 1987, a Senate resolution condemning Noriega was opposed by Elliott Abrams, the State Department official in charge of US policy in Central America and Panama.

And yet, when Noriega was finally indicted in Miami in 1988, all the charges except one were related to activities that took place *before* 1984—back when he was our boy, helping with the US war against Nicaragua, stealing elections with US approval and generally serving US interests satisfactorily. It had nothing to do with suddenly discovering that he was a gangster and a drug-peddler—that was known all along.

It's all quite predictable, as study after study shows. A brutal tyrant crosses the line from admirable friend to "villain" and "scum" when he commits the crime of independence. One common mistake is to go beyond robbing the poor—which is just fine—and to start interfering with the privileged, eliciting opposition from business leaders.

By the mid 1980s, Noriega was guilty of these crimes. Among other things, he seems to have been dragging his feet about helping the US in the contra war. His independence also threatened our interests in the Panama Canal. On January 1, 1990, most of the administration of the Canal was due to go over to Panama—in the year 2000, it goes completely to them. We had to make sure that Panama was in the hands of people we could control before that date.

Since we could no longer trust Noriega to do our bidding, he had to go. Washington imposed economic sanctions that virtually destroyed the economy, the main burden falling on the poor nonwhite majority. They too came to hate Noriega, not least because he was responsible for the economic warfare (which was illegal, if anyone cares) that was causing their children to starve.

Next a military coup was tried, but failed. Then, in December 1989, the US celebrated the fall of the Berlin wall and the end of the Cold War by invading Panama outright, killing hundreds or perhaps thousands of civilians (no one knows, and few north of the Rio Grande care enough to inquire). This restored power to the rich white elite that had been displaced by the Torrijos coup—just in time to ensure a compliant government for the administrative changeover of the Canal on January 1, 1990 (as noted by the right-wing European press).

Throughout this process, the US press followed Washington's lead, selecting villains in terms of current needs. Actions we'd formerly condoned became crimes. For example, in 1984, the Panamanian presidential election had been won by Arnulfo Arias. The election was stolen by Noriega, with considerable violence and fraud.

But Noriega hadn't yet become disobedient. He was our man in Panama, and the Arias party was considered to have dangerous elements of "ultranationalism." The Reagan administration therefore applauded the violence and fraud, and sent Secretary of State George Shultz down to legitimate the stolen election and praise Noriega's version of "democracy" as a model for the errant Sandinistas.

The Washington-media alliance and the major journals refrained from criticizing the fraudulent elections, but dismissed as utterly worthless the Sandinistas' far more free and honest election in the same year—because it could not be controlled.

In May 1989, Noriega again stole an election, this time from a representative of the business opposition, Guillermo Endara. Noriega used less violence than in 1984. But the Reagan administration had given the signal that it had turned against Noriega. Following the predictable script, the press expressed outrage over his failure to meet our lofty democratic standards.

The press also began passionately denouncing human rights violations that previously didn't reach the threshold of their attention. By the time we invaded Panama in December 1989, the press had demonized Noriega, turning him into the worst monster since Attila the Hun. (It was basically a replay of the demonization of Qaddafi of Libya.) Ted Koppel was orating that "Noriega belongs to that special fraternity of international villains, men like Qaddafi, Idi Amin and the Ayatollah Khomeini, whom Americans just love to hate." Dan Rather placed him "at the top of the list of the world's drug thieves and scums." In fact, Noriega remained a very minor thug—exactly what he was when he was on the CIA payroll.

In 1988, for example, *Americas Watch* published a report on human rights in Panama, giving an unpleasant picture. But as their reports—and other inquiries—make clear, Noriega's human rights record was nothing remotely like that of other US clients in the region, and no worse than in the days when Noriega was still a favorite, following orders.

Take Honduras, for example. Although it's not a murderous terrorist state like El Salvador or Guatemala, human rights abuses were probably worse there than in Panama. In fact, there's one CIA-trained battalion in Honduras that all by itself had carried out more atrocities than Noriega did.

Or consider US-backed dictators like Trujillo in the Dominican Republic, Somoza in Nicaragua, Marcos in the Philippines, Duvalier in Haiti and a host of Central American gangsters through the 1980s. They were all *much* more brutal than Noriega, but the United States supported them enthusiastically right through decades of horrifying atrocities—as long as the profits were flowing out of their countries and into the US. George Bush's administration continued to honor Mobutu, Ceausescu and Saddam Hussein, among others, all far worse criminals than Noriega. Suharto of Indonesia, arguably the worst killer of them all, remains a Washington-media "moderate."

In fact, at exactly the moment it invaded Panama because of its outrage over Noriega's abuses of human rights, the Bush administration announced new high-technology sales to China, noting that $300 million in business for US firms was at stake and that contacts had secretly resumed a few weeks after the Tiananmen Square massacre.

On the same day—the day Panama was invaded—the White House also announced plans (and implemented them shortly afterwards) to lift a ban on loans to Iraq. The State Department explained with a straight face that this was to achieve the "goal of increasing US exports and put us in a better position to deal with Iraq regarding its human rights record...."

The Department continued with the pose as Bush rebuffed the Iraqi democratic opposition (bankers, professionals, etc.) and blocked congressional efforts to condemn the atrocious crimes of his old friend Saddam Hussein. Compared to Bush's buddies in Baghdad and Beijing, Noriega looked like Mother Teresa.

After the invasion, Bush announced a billion dollars in aid to Panama. Of this, $400 million consisted of incentives for US business to export products to Panama, $150 million was to pay off bank loans and $65 million went to private sector loans and guarantees to US investors. In other words, about half the aid was a gift from the American taxpayer to American businesses.

The US put the bankers back in power after the invasion. Noriega's involvement in drug trafficking had been trivial compared to theirs. Drug trafficking there has always been conducted primarily by the banks—the banking system is virtually unregulated, so it's a natural outlet for criminal money. This has been the basis for Panama's highly artificial economy and remains so—possibly at a higher level—after the invasion. The Panamanian Defense Forces have also been reconstructed with basically the same officers.

In general, everything's pretty much the same, only now more reliable servants are in charge. (The same is true of Grenada, which has become a major center of drug money laundering since the US invasion. Nicaragua, too, has become a significant conduit for drugs to the US market, after Washington's victory in the 1990 election. The pattern is standard—as is the failure to notice it.)

Inoculating Southeast Asia

The US wars in Indochina fall into the same general pattern. By 1948, the State Department recognized quite clearly that the Viet Minh, the anti-French resistance led by Ho Chi Minh, was *the* national movement of Vietnam. But the Viet Minh did not cede control to the local oligarchy. It favored independent development and ignored the interests of foreign investors.

There was fear the Viet Minh might succeed, in which case "the rot would spread" and the "virus" would "infect" the region, to adopt the language the planners used year after year after year. (Except for a few madmen and nitwits, none feared conquest—they were afraid of a positive example of successful development.)

What do you do when you have a virus? First you destroy it, then you inoculate potential victims, so that the disease does not spread. That's basically the US strategy in the Third World.

If possible, it's advisable to have the local military destroy the virus for you. If they can't, you have to move your own forces in. That's more costly, and it's ugly, but sometimes you have to do it. Vietnam was one of those places where we had to do it.

Right into the late 1960s, the US blocked all attempts at political settlement of the conflict, even those advanced by the Saigon generals. If there were a political settlement, there might be progress toward successful development outside of our influence—an unacceptable outcome.

Instead, we installed a typical Latin American-style terror state in South Vietnam, subverted the only free elections in the history of Laos because the wrong side won, and blocked elections in Vietnam because it was obvious the wrong side was going to win there too.

The Kennedy administration escalated the attack against South Vietnam from massive state terror to outright aggression. Johnson sent a huge expeditionary force to attack South Vietnam and expanded the war to all of Indochina. That destroyed the virus, all right— Indochina will be lucky if it recovers in a hundred years.

While the United States was extirpating the disease of independent development at its source in Vietnam, it also prevented its spread by supporting the Suharto takeover in Indonesia in 1965, backing the overthrow of Philippine democracy by Ferdinand Marcos in 1972, supporting martial law in South Korea and Thailand and so on.

Suharto's 1965 coup in Indonesia was particularly welcome to the West, because it destroyed the only mass-based political party there. That involved the slaughter, in a few months, of about 700,000 people, mostly landless peasants—"a gleam of light in Asia," as the leading thinker of the *New York Times*, James Reston, exulted, assuring his readers that the US had a hand in this triumph.

The West was very pleased to do business with Indonesia's new "moderate" leader, as the *Christian Science Monitor* described General Suharto, after he had washed some of the blood off his hands—meanwhile adding hundreds of thousands of corpses in East Timor and elsewhere. This spectacular mass murderer is "at heart benign," the respected London *Economist* assures us—doubtless referring to his attitude towards Western corporations.

After the Vietnam war was ended in 1975, the major policy goal of the US has been to maximize repression and suffering in the countries that were devastated by our violence. The degree of the cruelty is quite astonishing.

When the Mennonites tried to send pencils to Cambodia, the State Department tried to stop them. When Oxfam tried to send ten solar pumps, the reaction was the same. The same was true when religious groups tried to send shovels to Laos to dig up some of the unexploded shells left by American bombing.

When India tried to send 100 water buffalo to Vietnam to replace the huge herds that were destroyed by the American attacks—and remember, in this primitive country, water buffalo mean fertilizer, tractors, survival—the United States threatened to cancel Food for Peace aid. (That's one Orwell would have appreciated.) No degree of cruelty is too great for Washington sadists. The educated classes know enough to look the other way.

In order to bleed Vietnam, we've supported the Khmer Rouge indirectly through our allies, China and Thailand. The Cambodians have to pay with their blood so we can make sure there isn't any recovery in Vietnam. The Vietnamese have to be punished for having resisted US violence.

Contrary to what virtually everyone—left or right—says, the United States achieved its major objectives in Indochina. Vietnam was demolished. There's no danger that successful development there will provide a model for other nations in the region.

Of course, it wasn't a total victory for the US. Our larger goal was to reincorporate Indochina into the US-dominated global system, and that has not yet been achieved.

But our basic goal—the crucial one, the one that really counted—was to destroy the virus, and we did achieve that. Vietnam is a basket case, and the US is doing what it can to keep it that way. In October 1991, the US once again overrode the strenuous objections of its allies in Europe and Japan, and renewed the embargo and sanctions against Vietnam. The Third World must learn that no one dare raise their head. The global enforcer will persecute them relentlessly if they commit this unspeakable crime.

The Gulf War

The Gulf War illustrated the same guiding principles, as we see clearly if we lift the veil of propaganda.

When Iraq invaded Kuwait in August 1990, the UN Security Council immediately condemned Iraq and imposed severe sanctions on it. Why was the UN response so prompt and so unprecedently firm? The US government-media alliance had a standard answer.

First, it told us that Iraq's aggression was a unique crime, and thus merited a uniquely harsh reaction. "America stands where it always has—against aggression, against those who would use force to replace the rule of law"—so we were informed by President Bush, the invader of Panama and the only head of state condemned by the World Court for the "unlawful use of force" (in the Court's condemnation of the US attack against Nicaragua). The media and the educated classes dutifully repeated the lines spelled out for them by their Leader, collapsing in awe at the magnificence of his high principles.

Second, these same authorities proclaimed in a litany that the UN was now at last functioning as it was designed to do. They claimed that this was impossible before the end of the Cold War, when the UN was rendered ineffective by Soviet disruption and the shrill anti-Western rhetoric of the Third World.

Neither of these claims can withstand even a moment's scrutiny. The US wasn't upholding any high principle in the Gulf, nor was any other state. The reason for the unprecedented response to Saddam Hussein wasn't his brutal aggression—it was because he stepped on the wrong toes.

Saddam Hussein is a murderous gangster— exactly as he was before the Gulf War, when he was our friend and favored trading partner. His invasion of Kuwait was certainly an atrocity, but well within the range of many similar crimes conducted by the US and its allies, and nowhere near as terrible as some. For example, Indonesia's invasion and annexation of East Timor reached near-genocidal proportions, thanks to the decisive support of the US and its allies. Perhaps one-fourth of the 700,000 population were killed, a slaughter exceeding that of Pol Pot, relative to the population, in the same years.

Our ambassador to the UN at the time (and now Senator from New York), Daniel Moynihan, explained his achievement at the UN concerning East Timor: "The United States wished things to turn out as they did, and worked to bring this about. The Department of State desired that the United Nations prove utterly ineffective in whatever measures it undertook. This task was given to me, and I carried it forward with no inconsiderable success."

The Australian Foreign Minister justified his country's acquiescence to the invasion and annexation of East Timor (and Australia's participation with Indonesia in robbing Timor's rich oil reserves) by saying simply that "the world is a pretty unfair place, littered with examples of acquisition by force." When Iraq invaded Kuwait, however, his government issued a ringing declaration that "big countries cannot invade small neighbors and get away with it." No heights of cynicism trouble the equanimity of Western moralists.

As for the UN finally functioning as it was designed to, the facts are clear—but absolutely barred by the guardians of political correctness who control the means of expression with an iron hand. For many years, the UN has been blocked by the great powers, primarily the United States—not the Soviet Union or the Third World. Since 1970, the United States has vetoed *far* more Security Council resolutions than any other country (Britain is second, France a distant third and the Soviet Union fourth).

Our record in the General Assembly is similar. And the "shrill, anti-Western rhetoric" of the Third World commonly turns out to be a call to observe international law, a pitifully weak barrier against the depredations of the powerful.

The UN was able to respond to Iraq's aggression because—for once—the United States *allowed* it to. The unprecedented severity of the UN sanctions was the result of intense US pressure and threats. The sanctions had an unusually good chance of working, both because of their harsh-

ness and because the usual sanctions-busters—
the United States, Britain and France—would
have abided by them for a change.

But even after allowing sanctions, the US
immediately moved to close off the diplomatic
option by dispatching a huge military force to
the Gulf, joined by Britain and backed by the
family dictatorships that rule the Gulf's oil states,
with only nominal participation by others.

A smaller, deterrent force could have been kept
in place long enough for the sanctions to have
had a significant effect; an army of half a million
couldn't. The purpose of the quick military build-
up was to ward off the danger that Iraq might be
forced out of Kuwait by peaceful means.

Why was a diplomatic resolution so unattrac-
tive? Within a few weeks after the invasion of
Kuwait on August 2, the basic outlines for a
possible political settlement were becoming clear.
Security Council resolution 660, calling for Iraq's
withdrawal from Kuwait, also called for simulta-
neous negotiations of border issues. By mid-
August, the National Security Council considered an Iraqi proposal to withdraw from Kuwait
in that context.

There appear to have been two issues: first,
Iraqi access to the Gulf, which would have
entailed a lease or other control over two unin-
habited mudflats assigned to Kuwait by Britain
in its imperial settlement (which had left Iraq
virtually landlocked); second, resolution of a
dispute over an oil field that extended two miles
into Kuwait over an unsettled border.

The US flatly rejected the proposal, or any negotiations. On August 22, without revealing these facts about the Iraqi initiative (which it apparently knew), the *New York Times* reported that the Bush Administration was determined to block the "diplomatic track" for fear that it might "defuse the crisis" in very much this manner. (The basic facts were published a week later by the Long Island daily *Newsday*, but the media largely kept their silence.)

The last known offer before the bombing, released by US officials on January 2, 1991, called for total Iraqi withdrawal from Kuwait. There were no qualifications about borders, but the offer was made in the context of unspecified agreements on other "linked" issues: weapons of mass destruction in the region and the Israel-Arab conflict.

The latter issues include Israel's illegal occupation of southern Lebanon, in violation of Security Council resolution 425 of March 1978, which called for its immediate and unconditional withdrawal from the territory it had invaded. The US response was that there would be no diplomacy. The media suppressed the facts, *Newsday* aside, while lauding Bush's high principles.

The US refused to consider the "linked" issues because it was opposed to diplomacy on all the "linked" issues. This had been made clear months before Iraq's invasion of Kuwait, when the US had rejected Iraq's offer of negotiations over weapons of mass destruction. In the offer, Iraq proposed to destroy all such chemical and biological weapons, if other countries in the region also destroyed their weapons of mass destruction.

Saddam Hussein was then Bush's friend and ally, so he received a response, which was instructive. Washington said it welcomed Iraq's proposal to destroy its own weapons, but didn't want this linked to "other issues or weapons systems."

There was no mention of the "other weapons systems," and there's a reason for that. Israel not only may have chemical and biological weapons—it's also the only country in the Mideast with nuclear weapons (probably about 200 of them). But "Israeli nuclear weapons" is a phrase that can't be written or uttered by any official US government source. That phrase would raise the question of why all aid to Israel is not illegal, since foreign aid legislation from 1977 bars funds to any country that secretly develops nuclear weapons.

Independent of Iraq's invasion, the US had also always blocked any "peace process" in the Middle East that included an international conference and recognition of a Palestinian right of self-determination. For 20 years, the US has been virtually alone in this stance. UN votes indicate the regular annual pattern; once again in December 1990, right in the midst of the Gulf crisis, the call for an international conference was voted 144-2 (US and Israel). This had nothing to do with Iraq and Kuwait.

The US also adamantly refused to allow a reversal of Iraq's aggression by the peaceful means prescribed by international law. Instead it preferred to avoid diplomacy and to restrict the conflict to the arena of violence, in which a superpower facing no deterrent is bound to prevail over a Third World adversary.

As already discussed, the US regularly carries out or supports aggression, even in cases far more criminal than Iraq's invasion of Kuwait. Only the most dedicated commissar can fail to understand these facts, or the fact that in the rare case when the US happens to oppose some illegal act by a client or ally, it's quite happy with "linkage."

Take the South African occupation of Namibia, declared illegal by the World Court and the UN in the 1960s. The US pursued "quiet diplomacy" and "constructive engagement" for years, brokering a settlement that gave South Africa ample reward (including Namibia's major port) for its aggression and atrocities, with "linkage" extending to the Caribbean and welcome benefits for international business interests.

The Cuban forces that had defended Namibia's neighbor Angola from South African attack were withdrawn. Much as in Nicaragua after the 1987 "peace accords," the US continued to support the terrorist army backed by the US and its allies (South Africa and Zaire) and is preparing the ground for a 1992 Nicaragua-style "democratic election," where people will go to the polls under threat of economic strangulation and terrorist attack if they vote the wrong way.

Meanwhile, South Africa was looting and destroying Namibia, and using it as a base for violence against its neighbors. In the Reagan-Bush years (1980–1988) alone, South African violence led to about $60 billion in damage and over a million and a half people killed in the neighboring countries (excluding Namibia and South Africa). But the commissar class was unable to see these facts, and hailed George Bush's amazing display of principle as he opposed "linkage"—when someone steps on our toes.

More generally, opposing "linkage" amounts to little more than rejecting diplomacy, which always involves broader issues. In the case of Kuwait, the US position was particularly flimsy. After Saddam Hussein stepped out of line, the Bush administration insisted that Iraq's capacity for aggression be eliminated (a correct position, in contrast to its earlier support for Saddam's aggression and atrocities) and called for a regional settlement guaranteeing security.

Well, that's linkage. The simple fact is that the US feared that diplomacy might "defuse the crisis," and therefore blocked diplomacy "linkage" at every turn during the build-up to the war.

By refusing diplomacy, the US achieved its major goals in the Gulf. We were concerned that the incomparable energy resources of the Middle East remain under our control, and that the enormous profits they produce help support the economies of the US and its British client.

The US also reinforced its dominant position, and taught the lesson that the world is to be ruled by force. Those goals having been achieved, Washington proceeded to maintain "stability," barring any threat of democratic change in the Gulf tyrannies and lending tacit support to Saddam Hussein as he crushed the popular uprising of the Shi'ites in the South, a few miles from US lines, and then the Kurds in the North.

But the Bush administration has not yet succeeded in achieving what its spokesman at the

New York Times, chief diplomatic correspondent Thomas Friedman, calls "the best of all worlds: an iron-fisted Iraqi junta without Saddam Hussein." This, Friedman writes, would be a return to the happy days when Saddam's "iron fist...held Iraq together, much to the satisfaction of the American allies Turkey and Saudi Arabia," not to speak of the boss in Washington. The current situation in the Gulf reflects the priorities of the superpower that held all the cards, another truism that must remain invisible to the guardians of the faith.

The Iran/contra cover-up

The major elements of the Iran/contra story were well known long before the 1986 exposures, apart from one fact: that the sale of arms to Iran via Israel and the illegal contra war run out of Ollie North's White House office were connected.

The shipment of arms to Iran through Israel didn't begin in 1985, when the congressional inquiry and the special prosecutor pick up the story. It began almost immediately after the fall of the Shah in 1979. By 1982, it was public knowledge that Israel was providing a large part of the arms for Iran—you could read it on the front page of the *New York Times.*

In February 1982, the main Israeli figures whose names later appeared in the Iran/contra hearings appeared on BBC television and described how they had helped organize an arms flow to the Khomeini regime. In October 1982, the Israeli ambassador to the US stated publicly that Israel was sending arms to the Khomeini regime "with the cooperation of the United States...at almost the highest level." The high Israeli officials involved also gave the reasons: to establish links with elements of the military in Iran who might overthrow the regime, restoring the arrangements that prevailed under the Shah—standard operating procedure.

As for the contra war, the basic facts of the illegal North-CIA operations were known by 1985 (over a year before the story broke, when a US supply plane was shot down and a US agent, Eugene Hasenfus, was captured). The media simply chose to look the other way.

So what finally generated the Iran/contra scandal? A moment came when it was just impossible to suppress it any longer. When Hasenfus was shot down in Nicaragua while flying arms to the contras for the CIA, and the Lebanese press reported that the US National Security Adviser was handing out Bibles and chocolate cakes in Teheran, the story just couldn't be kept under wraps. After that, the connection between the two well-known stories emerged.

We then move to the next phase: damage control. That's what the follow-up was about.

The prospects for Eastern Europe

What was remarkable about the events in Eastern Europe in the 1980s was that the imperial power simply backed off. Not only did the USSR permit popular movements to function, it actually encouraged them. There are few historical precedents for that.

It didn't happen because the Soviets are nice guys—they were driven by internal necessities. But it *did* happen and, as a result, the popular movements in Eastern Europe didn't have to face anything remotely like what they would have faced on our turf. The journal of the Salvadoran Jesuits quite accurately pointed out that in their country Vaclav Havel (the former political prisoner who became president of Czechoslovakia) wouldn't have been put in jail—he might well have been hacked to pieces and left by the side of the road somewhere.

The USSR even apologized for its past use of violence, and this too was unprecedented. US newspapers concluded that, because the Russians admitted that the invasion of Afghanistan was a crime that violated international law, they were finally joining the civilized world. That's an interesting reaction. Imagine someone in the US media suggesting that maybe the United States ought to try to rise to the moral level of the Kremlin and admit that the attacks against Vietnam, Laos and Cambodia violated international law.

The one country in Eastern Europe where there was extensive violence as the tyrannies collapsed was the very one where the Soviets had the least amount of influence and where we had the most: Romania. Nicolae Ceausescu, the dictator of Romania, had visited England and was given the royal treatment. The United States gave him favored nation treatment, trade advantages and the like.

Ceausescu was just as brutal and crazed then as he was later, but because he'd largely withdrawn from the Warsaw Pact and was following a somewhat independent course, we felt he was partially on our side in the international struggle. (We're in favor of independence as long as it's in *other* people's empires, not in our own.)

Elsewhere in Eastern Europe, the uprisings were remarkably peaceful. There was some repression, but historically, 1989 was unique. I can't think of another case that comes close to it.

I think the prospects are pretty dim for Eastern Europe. The West has a plan for it—they want to turn large parts of it into a new, easily exploitable part of the Third World.

There used to be a sort of colonial relationship between Western and Eastern Europe; in fact, the Russians' blocking of that relationship was one of the reasons for the Cold War. Now it's being reestablished and there's a serious conflict over who's going to win the race for robbery and exploitation. Is it going to be German-led Western Europe (currently in the lead) or Japan (waiting in the wings to see how good the profits look) or the United States (trying to get into the act)?

There are a lot of resources to be taken, and lots of cheap labor for assembly plants. But first we have to impose the capitalist model on them. We don't accept it for *ourselves*—but for the Third World, we insist on it. That's the IMF system. If we can get them to accept that, they'll be very easily exploitable, and will move toward their new role as a kind of Brazil or Mexico.

In many ways, Eastern Europe is more attractive to investors than Latin America. One reason is that the population is white and blue-eyed, and therefore easier to deal with for investors who come from deeply racist societies like Western Europe and the United States.

More significantly, Eastern Europe has much higher general health and educational standards than Latin America—which, except for isolated sectors of wealth and privilege, is a total disaster area. One of the few exceptions in this regard is Cuba, which does approach Western standards of health and literacy, but its prospects are very grim.

One reason for this disparity between Eastern Europe and Latin America is the vastly greater level of state terror in the latter after the Stalin years. A second reason is economic policy.

According to US intelligence, the Soviet Union poured about 80 billion dollars into Eastern Europe in the 1970s. The situation has been quite different in Latin America. Between 1982 and 1987, about 150 billion dollars were transferred *from* Latin America to the West. The *New York Times* cites estimates that "hidden transactions" (including drug money, illegal profits, etc.) might be in the 700 billion range. The effects in Central America have been particularly awful, but the same is true throughout Latin America—there's rampant poverty, malnutrition, infant mortality, environmental destruction, state terror, and a collapse of living standards to the levels of decades ago.

The situation in Africa is even worse. The catastrophe of capitalism was particularly severe in the 1980s, an "unrelenting nightmare" in the domains of the Western powers, in the accurate terms of the head of the Organization of African Unity. Illustrations provided by the World Health Organization estimate that eleven million children die every year in "the developing world," a "silent genocide" that could be brought to a quick end if resources were directed to human needs rather than enrichment of a few.

In a global economy designed for the interests and needs of international corporations and finance, and sectors that serve them, most of the species becomes superfluous. They will be cast aside if the institutional structures of power and privilege function without popular challenge or control.

The world's rent-a-thug

For most of this century, the United States was far and away the world's dominant economic power, and that made economic warfare an appealing weapon, including measures ranging from illegal embargo to enforcement of IMF rules (for the weak). But in the last twenty years or so, the US has declined relative to Japan and German-led Europe (thanks in part to the economic mismanagement of the Reagan administration, which threw a party for the rich with costs paid by the majority of the population and future generations). At the same time, however, US military power has become absolutely preeminent.

As long as the Soviet Union was in the game, there was a limit to how much force the US could apply, particularly in more remote areas where we didn't have a big conventional force advantage. Because the USSR used to support governments and political movements the US was trying to destroy, there was a danger that US intervention in the Third World might explode into a nuclear war. With the Soviet deterrent gone, the US is much more free to use violence around the world, a fact that has been recognized with much satisfaction by US policy analysts in the past several years.

In any confrontation, each participant tries to shift the battle to a domain in which it's most likely to succeed. You want to lead with your strength, play your strong card. The strong card of the United States is force—so if we can establish the principle that force rules the world, that's a victory for us. If, on the other hand, a conflict is settled through peaceful means, that benefits us less, because our rivals are just as good or better in that domain.

Diplomacy is a particularly unwelcome option, unless it's pursued under the gun. The US has very little popular support for its goals in the Third World. This isn't surprising, since it's trying to impose structures of domination and exploitation. A diplomatic settlement is bound to respond, at least to some degree, to the interests of the other participants in the negotiation, and that's a problem when your positions aren't very popular.

As a result, negotiations are something the US commonly tries to avoid. Contrary to much propaganda, that has been true in Southeast Asia, the Middle East and Central America for many years.

Against this background, it's natural that the Bush administration should regard military force as a major policy instrument, preferring it to sanctions and diplomacy (as in the Gulf crisis). But since the US now lacks the economic base to impose "order and stability" in the Third World, it must rely on others to pay for the exercise—a necessary one, it's widely assumed, since someone must ensure a proper respect for the masters. The flow of profits from Gulf oil production helps, but Japan and German-led continental Europe must also pay their share as the US adopts the "mercenary role," following the advice of the international business press.

The financial editor of the conservative *Chicago Tribune* has been stressing these themes with particular clarity. We must be "willing mercenaries," paid for our ample services by our rivals, using our "monopoly power" in the "security market" to maintain "our control over the world economic system." We should run a global protection racket, he advises, selling "protection" to other wealthy powers who will pay us a "war premium."

This is Chicago, where the words are understood: if someone bothers you, you call on the Mafia to break their bones. And if you fall behind in your premium, your health may suffer too.

To be sure, the use of force to control the Third World is only a last resort. The IMF is a more cost-effective instrument than the Marines and the CIA if it can do the job. But the "iron fist" must be poised in the background, available when needed.

Our rent-a-thug role also causes suffering at home. All of the successful industrial powers have relied on the state to protect and enhance powerful domestic economic interests, to direct public resources to the needs of investors, and so on—one reason why they are successful. Since 1950, the US has pursued these ends largely through the Pentagon system (including NASA and the Department of Energy, which produces nuclear weapons). By now we are locked into these devices for maintaining electronics, computers and high-tech industry generally.

Reaganite military Keynesian excesses added further problems. The transfer of resources to wealthy minorities and other government policies led to a vast wave of financial manipulations and a consumption binge. But there was little in the way of productive investment, and the country was saddled with huge debts: government, corporate, household and the incalculable debt of unmet social needs as the society drifts towards a Third World pattern, with islands of great wealth and privilege in a sea of misery and suffering.

When a state is committed to such policies, it must somehow find a way to divert the population, to keep them from seeing what's happening around them. There are not many ways to do this. The standard ones are to inspire fear of terrible enemies about to overwhelm us, and awe for our grand leaders who rescue us from disaster in the nick of time.

That has been the pattern right through the 1980s, requiring no little ingenuity as the standard device, the Soviet threat, became harder to take seriously. So the threat to our existence has been Qaddafi and his hordes of international terrorists, Grenada and its ominous air base, Sandinistas marching on Texas, Hispanic narcotraffickers led by the arch-maniac Noriega, and crazed Arabs generally. Most recently it's Saddam Hussein, after he committed his sole crime—the crime of disobedience—in August 1990. It has become more necessary to recognize what has always been true: that the prime enemy is the Third World, which threatens to get "out of control."

These are not laws of nature. The processes, and the institutions that engender them, could be changed. But that will require cultural, social and institutional changes of no little moment, including democratic structures that go far beyond periodic selection of representatives of the business world to manage domestic and international affairs.

Brainwashing at home

How the Cold War worked

Despite much pretense, national security has not been a major concern of US planners and elected officials. The historical record reveals this clearly. Few serious analysts took issue with George Kennan's position that "it is not Russian military power which is threatening us, it is Russian political power" (October 1947); or with President Eisenhower's consistent view that the Russians intended no military conquest of Western Europe and that the major role of NATO was to "convey a feeling of confidence to exposed populations, a confidence which will make them sturdier, politically, in their opposition to Communist inroads."

Similarly, the US dismissed possibilities for peaceful resolution of the Cold War conflict, which would have left the "political threat" intact. In his history of nuclear weapons, McGeorge Bundy writes that he is "aware of no serious contemporary proposal...that ballistic missiles should somehow be banned by agreement before they were ever deployed," even though these were the only potential military threat to the US. It was always the "political" threat of so-called "Communism" that was the primary concern.

(Recall that "Communism" is a broad term, and includes all those with the "ability to get control of mass movements....something we have no capacity to duplicate," as Secretary of State

John Foster Dulles privately complained to his brother Allen, CIA director, "The poor people are the ones they appeal to," he added, "and they have always wanted to plunder the rich." So they must be overcome, to protect our doctrine that the rich should plunder the poor.)

Of course, both the US and USSR would have preferred that the other simply disappear. But since this would obviously have involved mutual annihilation, a system of global management called the Cold War was established.

According to the conventional view, the Cold War was a conflict between two superpowers, caused by Soviet aggression, in which we tried to contain the Soviet Union and protect the world from it. If this view is a doctrine of theology, there's no need to discuss it. If it is intended to shed some light on history, we can easily put it to the test, bearing in mind a very simple point: if you want to understand the Cold War, you should look at the *events* of the Cold War. If you do so, a very different picture emerges.

On the Soviet side, the events of the Cold War were repeated interventions in Eastern Europe: tanks in East Berlin and Budapest and Prague. These interventions took place along the route that was used to attack and virtually destroy Russia three times in this century alone. The invasion of Afghanistan is the one example of an intervention outside that route, though also on the Soviet border.

On the US side, intervention was worldwide, reflecting the status attained by the US as the first truly global power in history.

On the domestic front, the Cold War helped the Soviet Union entrench its military-bureaucratic ruling class in power, and it gave the US a way to compel its population to subsidize high-tech industry. It isn't easy to sell all that to the domestic populations. The technique used was the old stand-by—fear of a great enemy.

The Cold War provided that too. No matter how outlandish the idea that the Soviet Union and its tentacles were strangling the West, the "Evil Empire" *was* in fact evil, *was* an empire and *was* brutal. Each superpower controlled its primary enemy—its own population—by terrifying it with the (quite real) crimes of the other.

In crucial respects, then, the Cold War was a kind of tacit arrangement between the Soviet Union and the United States under which the US conducted its wars against the Third World and controlled its allies in Europe, while the Soviet rulers kept an iron grip on their own internal empire and their satellites in Eastern Europe—each side using the other to justify repression and violence in its own domains.

So why did the Cold War end, and how does its end change things? By the 1970s, Soviet military expenditures were leveling off and internal problems were mounting, with economic stagnation and increasing pressures for an end to tyrannical rule. Soviet power internationally had, in fact, been declining for some 30 years, as a study by the Center for Defense Information showed in 1980. A few years later, the Soviet system had collapsed. The Cold War ended with the victory of what had always been the far richer and more powerful contestant. The Soviet collapse was part of the more general economic catastrophe of the 1980s, more severe in most of the Third World domains of the West than in the Soviet empire.

As we've already seen, the Cold War had significant elements of North-South conflict (to use the contemporary euphemism for the European conquest of the world). Much of the Soviet empire had formerly been quasi-colonial dependencies of the West. The Soviet Union took an independent course, providing assistance to targets of Western attack and deterring the worst of Western violence. With the collapse of Soviet tyranny, much of the region can be expected to return to its traditional status, with the former higher echelons of the bureaucracy playing the role of the Third World elites that enrich themselves while serving the interests of foreign investors.

But while this particular phase has ended, North-South conflicts continue. One side may have called off the game, but the US is proceeding as before—more freely, in fact, with Soviet deterrence a thing of the past. It should have surprised no one that George Bush celebrated the symbolic end of the Cold War, the fall of the Berlin Wall, by immediately invading Panama and announcing loud and clear that the US would subvert Nicaragua's election by maintaining its economic stranglehold and military attack unless "our side" won.

Nor did it take great insight for Elliott Abrams to observe that the US invasion of Panama was unusual because it could be conducted without fear of a Soviet reaction anywhere, or for numerous commentators during the Gulf crisis to add that the US and Britain were now free to use unlimited force against its Third World enemy, since they were no longer inhibited by the Soviet deterrent.

Of course, the end of the Cold War brings its problems too. Notably, the technique for controlling the domestic population has had to shift, a problem recognized through the 1980s, as we've already seen. New enemies have to be invented. It becomes harder to disguise the fact that the real enemy has always been "the poor who seek to plunder the rich"—in particular, Third World miscreants who seek to break out of the service role.

The war on (certain) drugs

One substitute for the disappearing Evil Empire has been the threat of drug traffickers from Latin America. In early September 1989, a major government-media blitz was launched by the President. That month the AP wires carried more stories about drugs than about Latin America, Asia, the Middle East and Africa combined. If you looked at television, every news program had a big section on how drugs were destroying our society, becoming the greatest threat to our existence, etc.

The effect on public opinion was immediate. When Bush won the 1988 election, people said the budget deficit was the biggest problem facing the country. Only about 3% named drugs. After the media blitz, concern over the budget was way down and drugs had soared to about 40% or 45%, which is highly unusual for an open question (where no specific answers are suggested).

Now, when some client state complains that the US government isn't sending it enough money, they no longer say, "we need it to stop the Russians"—rather, "we need it to stop drug trafficking." Like the Soviet threat, this enemy provides a good excuse for a US military presence where there's rebel activity or other unrest.

So internationally, "the war on drugs" provides a cover for intervention. Domestically, it has little to do with drugs but a lot to do with distracting the population, increasing repression in the inner cities, and building support for the attack on civil liberties.

That's not to say that "substance abuse" isn't a serious problem. At the time the drug war was launched, deaths from tobacco were estimated at about 300,000 a year, with perhaps another 100,000 from alcohol. But these aren't the drugs the Bush administration targeted. It went after illegal drugs, which had caused many fewer deaths—over 3500 a year—according to official figures. One reason for going after these drugs was that their use had been declining for some years, so the Bush administration could safely predict that its drug war would "succeed" in lowering drug use.

The Administration also targeted marijuana, which hadn't caused any known deaths among some 60 million users. In fact, that crackdown has exacerbated the drug problem—many marijuana users have turned from this relatively harmless drug to more dangerous drugs like cocaine, which are easier to conceal.

Just as the drug war was launched with great fanfare in September 1989, the US Trade Representative (USTR) panel held a hearing in Washington to consider a tobacco industry request that the US impose sanctions on Thailand in retaliation for its efforts to restrict US tobacco imports and advertising. Such US government actions had already rammed this lethal addictive narcotic down the throats of consumers in Japan, South Korea and Taiwan, with human costs of the kind already indicated

The US Surgeon General, Everett Koop, testified at the USTR panel that "when we are pleading with foreign governments to stop the flow of cocaine, it is the height of hypocrisy for the United States to export tobacco." He added, "years from now, our nation will look back on this application of free trade policy and find it scandalous."

Thai witnesses also protested, predicting that the consequence of US sanctions would be to reverse a decline in smoking achieved by their government's campaign against tobacco use. Responding to the US tobacco companies' claim that their product is the best in the world, a Thai witness said: "Certainly in the Golden Triangle we have some of the best products, but we never ask the principle of free trade to govern such products. In fact we suppressed [them]." Critics recalled the Opium War 150 years earlier, when the British government compelled China to open its doors to opium from British India, sanctimoniously pleading the virtues of free trade as they forcefully imposed large-scale drug addiction on China.

Here we have the biggest drug story of the day. Imagine the screaming headlines: "US government the world's leading drug peddler." It would surely sell papers. But the story passed virtually unreported, and with not a hint of the obvious conclusions.

Another aspect of the drug problem, which also received little attention, is the leading role of the US government in stimulating drug trafficking since World War II. This happened in part when the US began its postwar task of undermining the anti-fascist resistance and the labor movement became an important target.

In France, the threat of the political power and influence of the labor movement was enhanced by its steps to impede the flow of arms to French forces seeking to reconquer their former colony of Vietnam with US aid. So the CIA undertook to weaken and split the French labor movement— with the aid of top American labor leaders, who were quite proud of their role.

The task required strikebreakers and goons. There was an obvious supplier: the Mafia. Of course, they didn't take on this work just for the fun of it. They wanted a return for their efforts. And it was given to them: they were authorized to reestablish the heroin racket that had been suppressed by the fascist governments—the famous "French connection" that dominated the drug trade until the 1960s.

By then, the center of the drug trade had shifted to Indochina, particularly Laos and Thailand. The shift was again a by-product of a CIA operation—the "secret war" fought in those countries during the Vietnam War by a CIA mercenary army. They also wanted a payoff for their contributions. Later, as the CIA shifted its activities to Pakistan and Afghanistan, the drug racket boomed there.

The clandestine war against Nicaragua also provided a shot in the arm to drug traffickers in the region, as illegal CIA arms flights to the US mercenary forces offered an easy way to ship drugs back to the US, sometimes through US Air Force bases, traffickers report.

The close correlation between the drug racket and international terrorism (sometimes called "counterinsurgency," "low intensity conflict" or some other euphemism) is not surprising. Clandestine operations need plenty of money, which should be undetectable. And they need criminal operatives as well. The rest follows.

War is Peace.
Freedom is Slavery.
Ignorance is Strength.

The terms of political discourse typically have two meanings. One is the dictionary meaning, and the other is a meaning that is useful for serving power—the doctrinal meaning.

Take *democracy*. According to the common-sense meaning, a society is democratic to the extent that people can participate in a meaningful way in managing their affairs. But the doctrinal meaning of *democracy* is different—it refers to a system in which decisions are made by sectors of the business community and related elites. The public are to be only "spectators of action," not "participants," as leading democratic theorists (in this case, Walter Lippmann) have explained. They are permitted to ratify the decisions of their betters and to lend their support to one or another of them, but not to interfere with matters—like public policy—that are none of their business.

If segments of the public depart from their apathy and begin to organize and enter the public arena, that's not democracy. Rather, it's a *crisis of democracy* in proper technical usage, a threat that has to be overcome in one or another way: in El Salvador, by death squads— at home, by more subtle and indirect means.

Or take *free enterprise*, a term that refers, in practice, to a system of public subsidy and private profit, with massive government intervention in the economy to maintain a welfare state for the rich. In fact, in acceptable usage, just about any phrase containing the word "free" is likely to mean something like the opposite of its actual meaning.

Or take *defense against aggression*, a phrase that's used—predictably—to refer to aggression. When the US attacked South Vietnam in the early 1960s, the liberal hero Adlai Stevenson (among others) explained that we were defending South Vietnam against "internal aggression"—that is, the aggression of South Vietnamese peasants against the US air force and a US-run mercenary army, which were driving them out of their homes and into concentration camps where they could be "protected" from the southern guerrillas. In fact, these peasants willingly supported the guerillas, while the US client regime was an empty shell, as was agreed on all sides.

So magnificently has the doctrinal system risen to its task that to this day, 30 years later, the idea that the US attacked South Vietnam is unmentionable, even unthinkable, in the mainstream. The essential issues of the war are, correspondingly, beyond any possibility of discussion now. The guardians of political correctness (the real PC) can be quite proud of an achievement that would be hard to duplicate in a well-run totalitarian state.

Or take the term *peace process*. The naive might think that it refers to efforts to seek peace. Under this meaning, we would say that the peace process in the Middle East includes, for example, the offer of a full peace treaty to Israel by President Sadat of Egypt in 1971, along lines advocated by virtually the entire world, including official US policy; the Security Council resolution of January 1976 introduced by the major Arab states with the backing of the PLO, which called for a two-state settlement of the Arab-Israel conflict in the terms of a near-universal international consensus; PLO offers through the 1980s to negotiate with Israel for mutual recognition; and annual votes at the UN General Assembly, most recently in December 1990 (voted 144–2), calling for an international conference on the Israel-Arab problem, etc.

But the sophisticated understand that these efforts do not form part of the peace process. The reason is that in the PC meaning, the term *peace process* refers to what the US government is doing—in the cases mentioned, this is to block international efforts to seek peace. The cases cited do not fall within the peace process, because the US backed Israel's rejection of Sadat's offer, vetoed the Security Council resolution, opposed negotiations and mutual recognition of the PLO and Israel, and regularly joins with Israel in opposing—thereby, in effect, vetoing—any attempt to move towards a peaceful diplomatic settlement at the UN or elsewhere.

The peace process is restricted to US initiatives, which call for a unilateral US-determined settlement with no recognition of Palestinian national rights. That's the way it works. Those who cannot master these skills must seek another profession.

There are many other examples. Take the term *special interest.* The well-oiled Republican PR systems of the 1980s regularly accused the Democrats of being the party of the special interests: women, labor, the elderly, the young, farmers—in short, the general population. There was only one sector of the population never listed as a special interest: corporations and business generally. That makes sense. In PC discourse their (special) interests are the *national interest,* to which all must bow.

The Democrats plaintively retorted that they were *not* the party of the special interests: they served the national interest too. That was correct, but their problem has been that they lack the single-minded class consciousness of their Republican opponents. The latter are not confused about their role as representatives of the owners and managers of the society, who are fighting a bitter class war against the general population—often adopting vulgar Marxist rhetoric and concepts, resorting to jingoist hysteria, fear and terror, awe of great leaders and the other standard devices of population control. The Democrats are less clear about their allegiances, hence less effective in the propaganda wars.

Finally, take the term *conservative,* which has come to refer to advocates of a powerful state, which interferes massively in the economy and in social life. They advocate huge state expenditures and a postwar peak of protectionist measures and insurance against market risk, narrowing individual liberties through legislation and court-packing, protecting the Holy State from unwarranted inspection by the irrelevant citizenry—in short, those programs that are the precise opposite of traditional conservatism. Their allegiance is to "the people who own the country" and therefore "ought to govern it," in the words of Founding Father John Jay.

It's really not that hard, once one understands the rules.

To make sense of political discourse, it's necessary to give a running translation into English, decoding the doublespeak of the media, academic social scientists and the secular priesthood generally. Its function is not obscure: the effect is to make it impossible to find words to talk about matters of human significance in a coherent way. We can then be sure that little will be understood about how our society works and what is happening in the world—a major contribution to *democracy*, in the PC sense of the word.

Socialism, real and fake

One can debate the meaning of the term "socialism," but if it means anything, it means control of production by the workers themselves, not owners and managers who rule them and control all decisions, whether in capitalist enterprises or an absolutist state.

To refer to the Soviet Union as *socialist* is an interesting case of doctrinal doublespeak. The Bolshevik coup of October 1917 placed state power in the hands of Lenin and Trotsky, who moved quickly to dismantle the incipient socialist institutions that had grown up during the popular revolution of the preceding months—the factory councils, the Soviets, in fact any organ of popular control—and to convert the workforce into what they called a "labor army" under the command of the leader. In any meaningful sense of the term "socialism," the Bolsheviks moved at once to destroy its existing elements. No socialist deviation has been permitted since.

These developments came as no surprise to leading Marxist intellectuals, who had criticized Lenin's doctrines for years (as had Trotsky) because they would centralize authority in the hands of the vanguard Party and its leaders. In fact, decades earlier, the anarchist thinker

Bakunin had predicted that the emerging intellectual class would follow one of two paths: either they would try to exploit popular struggles to take state power themselves, becoming a brutal and oppressive Red bureaucracy; or they would become the managers and ideologists of the state capitalist societies, if popular revolution failed. It was a perceptive insight, on both counts.

The world's two major propaganda systems did not agree on much, but they did agree on using the term *socialism* to refer to the immediate destruction of every element of socialism by the Bolsheviks. That's not too surprising. The Bolsheviks called their system *socialist* so as to exploit the moral prestige of socialism.

The West adopted the same usage for the opposite reason: to defame the feared libertarian ideals by associating them with the Bolshevik dungeon, to undermine the popular belief that there really might be progress towards a more just society with democratic control over its basic institutions and concern for human needs and rights.

If socialism is the tyranny of Lenin and Stalin, then sane people will say: *not for me.* And if that's the only alternative to corporate state capitalism, then many will submit to its authoritarian structures as the only reasonable choice.

With the collapse of the Soviet system, there's an opportunity to revive the lively and vigorous libertarian socialist thought that was not able to withstand the doctrinal and repressive assaults of the major systems of power. How large a hope that is, we cannot know. But at least one roadblock has been removed. In that sense, the disappearance of the Soviet Union is a small victory for socialism, much as the defeat of the fascist powers was.

The media

Whether they're called "liberal" or "conservative," the major media are large corporations, owned by and interlinked with even larger conglomerates. Like other corporations, they sell a product to a market. The market is advertisers—that is, other businesses. The product is audiences. For the elite media that set the basic agenda to which others adapt, the product is, furthermore, relatively privileged audiences.

So we have major corporations selling fairly wealthy and privileged audiences to other businesses. Not surprisingly, the picture of the world presented reflects the narrow and biased interests and values of the sellers, the buyers and the product.

Other factors reinforce the same distortion. The cultural managers (editors, leading columnists, etc.) share class interests and associations with state and business managers and other privileged sectors. There is, in fact, a regular flow of high-level people among corporations, government and media. Access to state authorities is important to maintain a competitive position; "leaks," for example, are often fabrications and deceit produced by the authorities with the cooperation of the media, who pretend they don't know.

In return, state authorities demand cooperation and submissiveness. Other power centers
also have devices to punish departures from
orthodoxy, ranging from the stock market to an
effective vilification and defamation apparatus.

The outcome is not, of course, entirely uni-
form. To serve the interests of the powerful, the
media must present a tolerably realistic picture
of the world. And professional integrity and
honesty sometimes interfere with the overriding
mission. The best journalists are, typically, quite
aware of the factors that shape the media product, and seek to use such openings as are
provided. The result is that one can learn a lot by
a critical and skeptical reading of what the
media produce.

The media are only one part of a larger doctrinal system; other parts are journals of opinion,
the schools and universities, academic scholar-
ship and so on. We're much more aware of the
media, particularly the prestige media, because
those who critically analyze ideology have fo-
cused on them. The larger system hasn't been
studied as much because it's harder to investi-
gate systematically. But there's good reason to
believe that it represents the same interests as
the media, just as one would anticipate.

The doctrinal system, which produces what
we call "propaganda" when discussing enemies,
has two distinct targets. One target is what's
sometimes called the "political class," the roughly
20% of the population that's relatively educated,
more or less articulate, playing some role in
decision-making. Their acceptance of doctrine

is crucial, because they're in a position to design and implement policy.

Then there's the other 80% or so of the population. These are Lippmann's "spectators of action," whom he referred to as the "bewildered herd." They are supposed to follow orders and keep out of the way of the important people. They're the target of the real *mass* media: the tabloids, the sitcoms, the Super Bowl and so on.

These sectors of the doctrinal system serve to divert the unwashed masses and reinforce the basic social values: passivity, submissiveness to authority, the overriding virtue of greed and personal gain, lack of concern for others, fear of real or imagined enemies, etc. The goal is to keep the bewildered herd bewildered. It's unnecessary for them to trouble themselves with what's happening in the world. In fact, it's undesirable—if they see too much of reality they may set themselves to change it.

That's not to say that the media can't be influenced by the general population. The dominant institutions—whether political, economic or doctrinal—are not immune to public pressures. Independent (alternative) media can also play an important role. Though they lack resources, almost by definition, they gain significance in the same way that popular organizations do: by bringing together people with limited resources who can multiply their effectiveness, and their own understanding, through their interactions—precisely the democratic threat that's so feared by dominant elites.

The future

Things have changed

It's important to recognize how much the scene has changed in the past 30 years as a result of the popular movements that organized in a loose and chaotic way around such issues as civil rights, peace, feminism, the environment and other issues of human concern.

Take the Kennedy and Reagan administrations, which were similar in a number of ways in their basic policies and commitments. When Kennedy launched a huge international terrorist campaign against Cuba after his invasion failed, and then escalated the murderous state terror in South Vietnam to outright aggression, there was no detectable protest.

It wasn't until hundreds of thousands of American troops were deployed and all of Indochina was under devastating attack, with hundreds of thousands slaughtered, that protest became more than marginally significant. In contrast, as soon as the Reagan administration hinted that they intended to intervene directly in Central America, spontaneous protest erupted at a scale sufficient to compel the state terrorists to turn to other means.

Leaders may crow about the end of the "Vietnam syndrome," but they know better. A National Security Policy Review of the Bush administration, leaked at the moment of the ground attack in the Gulf, noted that, "In cases where the US confronts much weaker enemies"—the only ones that the true statesman will agree to fight—"our challenge will be not simply to defeat them, but to defeat them decisively and rapidly." Any other outcome would be "embarrassing" and might "undercut political support," understood to be very thin.

By now, classical intervention is not even considered an option. The means are limited to clandestine terror, kept secret from the domestic population, or "decisive and rapid" demolition of "much weaker enemies"—after huge propaganda campaigns depicting them as monsters of indescribable power.

Much the same is true across the board. Take 1992. If the Columbus quincentenary had been in 1962, it would have been a celebration of the liberation of the continent. In 1992, that response no longer has a monopoly, a fact that has aroused much hysteria among the cultural managers who are used to near-totalitarian control. They now rant about the "fascist excesses" of those who urge respect for other people and other cultures.

In other areas too, there's more openness and understanding, more skepticism and questioning of authority. Of course, the latter tendencies are double-edged. They may lead to independent thought, popular organizing and pressures for much-needed institutional change. Or they may provide a mass base of frightened people for new authoritarian leaders. These possible outcomes are not a matter for speculation, but for action, with stakes that are very large.

What you can do

In any country, there's some group that has the real power. It's not a big secret where power is in the United States. It basically lies in the hands of the people who determine investment decisions—what's produced, what's distributed. They staff the government, by and large, choose the planners, and set the general conditions for the doctrinal system.

One of the things they want is a passive, quiescent population. So one of the things that you can do to make life uncomfortable for them is *not* be passive and quiescent. There are lots of ways of doing that. Even just asking questions can have an important effect.

Demonstrations, writing letters and voting can all be meaningful—it depends on the situation. But the main point is—it's got to be sustained and organized.

If you go to one demonstration and then go home, that's something, but the people in power can live with that. What they can't live with is sustained pressure that keeps building, organizations that keep doing things, people that keep learning lessons from the last time and doing it better the next time.

Any system of power, even a fascist dictatorship, is responsive to public dissidence. It's certainly true in a country like this, where—fortunately—the state doesn't have a lot of force to coerce people. During the Vietnam War, direct resistance to the war was quite significant, and it was a cost that the government had to pay.

If elections are just something in which some portion of the population goes and pushes a button every couple of years, they don't matter. But if the citizens organize to press a position, and pressure their representatives about it, elections can matter.

Members of the House of Representatives can be influenced much more easily than senators, and senators somewhat more easily than the president, who is usually immune. When you get to that level, policy is decided almost totally by the wealthy and powerful people who own and manage the country.

But you can organize on a scale that will influence representatives. You can get them to come to your homes to be yelled at by a group of neighbors, or you can sit in at their offices—whatever works in the circumstances. It can make a difference—often an important one.

You can also do your own research. Don't just rely on the conventional history books and political science texts—go back to specialists' monographs and to original sources: national security memoranda and similar documents. Most good libraries have reference departments where you can find them.

It does require a bit of effort. Most of the material is junk, and you have to read a ton of stuff before you find anything good. There are guides that give you hints about where to look, and sometimes you'll find references in secondary sources that look intriguing. Often they're misinterpreted, but they suggest places to search.

It's no big mystery, and it's not intellectually difficult. It involves some work, but anybody can do it as a spare-time job. And the results of that research can change people's minds. Real research is always a collective activity, and its results can make a large contribution to changing consciousness, increasing insight and understanding, and leading to constructive action.

The struggle continues

The struggle for freedom is never over. The people of the Third World need our sympathetic understanding and, much more than that, they need our help. We can provide them with a margin of survival by internal disruption in the United States. Whether they can succeed against the kind of brutality we impose on them depends in large part on what happens here.

The courage they show is quite amazing. I've personally had the privilege—and it is a privilege—of catching a glimpse of that courage at first hand in Southeast Asia, in Central America and on the occupied West Bank. It's a very moving and inspiring experience, and invariably brings to my mind some contemptuous remarks of Rousseau's on Europeans who have abandoned freedom and justice for the peace and repose "they enjoy in their chains." He goes on to say:

> When I see multitudes of entirely naked savages scorn European voluptuousness and endure hunger, fire, the sword and death to preserve only their independence, I feel that it does not behoove slaves to reason about freedom.

People who think that these are mere words understand very little about the world.

And that's just a part of the task that lies before us. There's a growing Third World at home. There are systems of illegitimate authority in every corner of the social, political, economic and cultural worlds. For the first time in human history, we have to face the problem of protecting an environment that can sustain a decent human existence. We don't know that honest and dedicated effort will be enough to solve or even mitigate such problems as these. We can be quite confident, however, that the lack of such efforts will spell disaster.

Political books by Noam Chomsky

Deterring Democracy. Routledge, Chapman & Hall, 1991; Verso (29 W 35th St, NYC 10001, 212 244 3336), 1991.

Necessary Illusions: Thought Control in Democratic Societies. South End Press (116 St Botolph St, Boston MA 02115; 617 266 0629), 1989.

The Culture of Terrorism. South End, 1988.

On Power and Ideology: the Managua Lectures. South End, 1987.

Pirates and Emperors: International Terrorism in the Real World. Black Rose Books (distributed by University of Toronto Press, 340 Nagel Dr, Cheektowaga NY 14225, 716 683 4547), 1987.

Turning the Tide: U.S. Intervention in Central America and the Struggle for Peace. South End, 1985.

The Fateful Triangle: the United States, Israel and the Palestinians. South End, 1983; Noontide, 1986.

Towards a New Cold War: Essays on the Current Crisis and How We Got There. Pantheon, 1982.

Radical Priorities. Black Rose, 1981.

For Reasons of State. Pantheon, 1973 (out of print).

At War with Asia. Pantheon, 1970 (out of print).

with Edward S. Herman

Manufacturing Consent: the Political Economy of the Mass Media. Pantheon, 1988.

After the Cataclysm: Postwar Indochina and the Reconstruction of Imperial Ideology. South End, 1979.

The Washington Connection and Third World Fascism. South End, 1979.

with others

Mobilizing Democracy: Changing the U.S. Role in the Middle East. Edited by Greg Bates. Common Courage (Box 702, Monroe ME 04951, 800 497 3207), 1991.

speeches

The New World Order. Open Magazine Pamphlet Series (Box 2726, Westfield NJ 07091; 908 789 9608), 1991.

Terrorizing the Neighborhood: American Foreign Policy in the Post-Cold War Era. Pressure Drop Press (Box 460754, San Francisco CA 94146), 1991.

U.S. Gulf Policy. Open Magazine Pamphlet Series, 1990.

Notes

Sources for the facts in this book are listed below by page numbers and brief subject descriptions. Full publication data is given the first time a work is cited—except for Chomsky's own books, which are described in the preceding section.

7–8. On "Grand Area" planning for the postwar period by the State Department and the CFR, see Laurence Shoup and William Minter, *Imperial Brain Trust,* Monthly Review, 1977. There is extensive literature on the development and execution of these plans. An early work, of great insight, is Gabriel Kolko, *Politics of War,*: Random House, 1968. One valuable recent study is Melvyn Leffler, *Preponderance of Power,* Stanford University Press, 1992. For further sources and discussion, specifically on NSC 68, see Chomsky, *Deterring Democracy,* Chapter 1. NSC 68 and many other declassified documents can be found in the official State Department history, *Foreign Relations of the United States,* generally published with about 30 years delay.

8–9. "Secret army." See Thomas Powers, *The Man Who Kept the Secrets: Richard Helms and the CIA,* Knopf, 1979; and Mary Ellen Reese, *General Reinhard Gehlen: the CIA Connection,* George Mason University Press, 1990. For further details, see Chomsky, *Turning the Tide* and sources cited; and Christopher Simpson, *Blowback,* Grove, Weidenfeld, 1987.

10. William Yandell Elliot, ed., *The Political Economy of American Foreign Policy,* Holt, Rinehart & Winston, 1955. For further discussion, see Chomsky, *At War with Asia,* Introduction.

10–11. Kennan, Latin America. See Walter LaFeber, *Inevitable Revolutions: the United States in Central America,* Norton, 1983.

11–18. Postwar planning. Chomsky, *Turning the Tide,* Chapters 2, 4; and *Deterring Democracy,* Chapters 1, 11 and sources cited.

15. Marshall Plan. See Michael J. Hogan, *The Marshall Plan,* Cambridge University Press, 1987.

18. Kolb. Letter, *New York Times,* July 26, 1983.

19. Ultranationalism quote. National Security Council Memorandum 5432, 1954.

19–20. US policy planners, Kennedy planners. See Chomsky, *On Power and Ideology,* Lecture 1.

20–21. Costa Rica, Dulles. Chomsky, *Necessary Illusions,* Appendix 5.1; Gordon Connell-Smith, *The Inter-American System,* Oxford University Press and Royal Institute of International Affairs, 1966.

25. "Stability." Peiro Gleijeses, *Shattered Hope,* Princeton University Press, 1991, 125, 365.

26–27. Japan, Kennan. Bruce Cumings, *The Origins of the Korean War,* Volume II, Princeton University Press, 1990.

28. Stimson. Kolko, *Politics of War,* 471.

29. Schoultz, Herman studies. Chomsky, *Turning the Tide,* 157f.

30. "Economic miracle." Chomsky, *Turning the Tide,* 1.8 and sources cited; Robert Williams, *Export Agriculture and the Crisis in Central America,* University of North Carolina Press, 1986.

30. Adams. Chomsky, *Deterring Democracy,* 34f.

31. Relations with the military. Chomsky, *On Power and Ideology,* Lecture 1 and *Turning the Tide,* 216.

31. US arms to Iran. Chomsky, *Fateful Triangle,* 475f; *Turning the Tide,* 130–31; and *Culture of Terrorism,* Chapter 8.

33. Brazil and the situation throughout the Third World. Chomsky, *Deterring Democracy,* Chapter 7; and South Commission, *The Challenge to the South,* Oxford University Press, 1990.

34–50. Central America. See Chomsky, *Turning the Tide; Culture of Terrorism; Necessary Illusions; Deterring Democracy;* Herman and Chomsky, *Manufacturing Consent.* See also John Hassett and Hugh Lacey, *Towards a Society that Serves its People: the Intellectual Contributions of El Salvador's Murdered Jesuits,* Georgetown University Press, 1992.

42. Oxfam's explanation. Dianna Melrose, *Nicaragua: the Threat of a Good Example,* Oxfam, 1985.

50–56. Panama. See Chomsky, *Deterring Democracy,* Chapter 5.

54. Bush's administration. Chomsky, "'What We Say Goes': The Middle East in the New World Order," in Cynthia Peters, ed., *Collateral Damage,* South End Press, 1992, 49-92.

56. Drugs. Chomsky, "Year 501: World Orders, Old and New, Part 1," *Z* magazine, March 1992, 24–36.

56–60. Southeast Asia and media coverage 1950s through mid-80s. Herman and Chomsky, *Manufacturing Consent.*

58. Media reaction to the Indonesia coup. Chomsky, "'A Gleam of Light in Asia,'" *Z* magazine, September 1990, 15–23.

60–68. Gulf War. Chomsky, *Deterring Democracy*, Chapter 6 and Afterword (1991 edition); and Chomsky, in Peters, *Collateral Damage*.

68–69. Iran/contra cover-up. Chomsky, *Fateful Triangle*, 475f; *Turning the Tide*, 130-131; and *Culture of Terrorism*, Chapter 8.

70. Salvadoran Jesuit journal. Chomsky, *Deterring Democracy*, 354–55.

72-73. Eastern Europe and Latin America; Africa. Chomsky, *Deterring Democracy*, Chapter 7.

75. *Chicago Tribune* quote. William Neikirk, "We are the World's Guardian Angels," *Chicago Tribune* business section, September 9, 1990. Cited in Chomsky, *Deterring Democracy*, 5.

78–82. The Cold War. Chomsky, *Turning the Tide*, Chapter 4; and *Deterring Democracy*.

79. Dulles quote. John Foster Dulles telephone call to Allen Dulles, June 19, 1958, "Minutes of Telephone Conversations of John Foster Dulles and Christian Herter," Dwight D. Eisenhower Library, Abilene Kansas. Cited in "A View from Below," *Diplomatic History*, Winter 1992.

82–86. War on drugs. Chomsky, *Deterring Democracy*, Chapter 4.

86–91. Political discourse. Edward S. Herman, *Beyond Hypocrisy*, South End Press, 1992.

87. Lipmann (and the evolution of these notions from 17th century England to today). Chomsky, *Deterring Democracy*. Chapter 12.

87. Stevenson; the concept "defense against aggression." Chomsky, *For Reasons of State*, Chapter 1, section 6.

88. "Peace process." Chomsky, *Towards a New Cold War*, Chapter 9; *Fateful Triangle*, Chapter 3; *Necessary Illusions*, Appendix 5.4; and *Deterring Democracy*, Afterword (1991 edition).

90. John Jay. Frank Monaghan, *John Jay*. New York: Bobbs-Merrill, 1935, p. 323.

91–92. Socialism. Herman and Chomsky, *Manufacturing Consent*.

96–97. National Security Policy Review. Maureen Dowd, *New York Times*, February 23, 1992.

Index